Praise for *Lead with Quiet Confidence*

"As an introvert myself, I found this book deeply resonant. Jennifer captures something many quiet leaders know in their bones: It can be hard to lead in environments that reward volume over thoughtfulness, even when you care deeply about people and love leading them. What makes this book so valuable is that it is not just affirming—it is practical, offering real tools for growth, from 'kind goals' and the LEAD framework to concrete guidance on speaking up, building visibility, and managing energy without losing your authenticity. *Lead with Quiet Confidence* is a powerful book because it will help unlock extraordinary talent and potential in people whose wisdom, calm, and insight have too often gone unseen."

—Jared Spataro, chief marketing officer,
AI at Work, Microsoft

"*Lead with Quiet Confidence* beautifully reframes introversion as a potential source of deep wisdom and authentic power. Jennifer Marcou offers a science-informed, compassionate guide that helps quiet leaders step into their purpose—not by becoming someone else, but by becoming more fully themselves. This book gives introverts the practical tools to transform self-doubt into grounded confidence and meaningful action."

—Scott Barry Kaufman, cognitive scientist,
podcaster, coach, and author of *Transcend*

"Throughout my career, I've seen that the quietest people in the room are often the ones with the most meaningful insights. They listen deeply, process thoughtfully, and connect ideas others may miss—bringing informed perspective where others may bring mere opinion. In *Lead with Quiet Confidence*, Jennifer Marcou offers practical, actionable guidance to help introverted professionals share those insights with clarity and strength. She empowers readers to lead authentically, contribute more fully, and grow their influence without compromising authenticity. As an introvert myself, I only wish I'd had access to this wisdom earlier in my career—and I'm grateful for a resource that will help today's quiet leaders find and own their voice."

—Susan Sobbott, former president, Global
Commercial Services, American Express

"As an introverted founder and leader, I've found that most workplaces are still designed around extroverted norms. Jennifer Marcou's blend of lived experience and research-backed coaching makes a powerful case that you don't need to change who you are to thrive and reach your full potential. This book reinforced something I've come to believe deeply: the most effective leaders aren't the loudest, but the ones who create space for others to grow and do their best work. *Lead with Quiet Confidence* is a must-read for any introvert who wants to lead with real impact while staying true to themselves."

—Eugen Neiculescu, cofounder and
chief experience officer, Adore Me

"This is the book so many introverts have been waiting for. Instead of telling you to speak louder or be more outgoing, Jennifer Marcou shows you how to succeed by working *with* your nature, not against it. *Lead with Quiet Confidence* is both practical and deeply affirming. It will help you reclaim your voice, trust your instincts, and lead in a way that feels authentic."

—Michaela Chung, author of *The Irresistible Introvert:
Harness the Power of Quiet Charisma in a Loud World*

"In fast-moving environments where ideas fuel innovation, *Lead with Quiet Confidence* shines a light on the often overlooked strengths of introverted employees. Jennifer Marcou provides a thoughtful, research-aligned guide for helping these individuals influence effectively and bring their best work forward. Any leader who cares about cultivating diverse creative talent will find tremendous value in this book."

—Chris Capossela, former executive vice president
and chief marketing officer, Microsoft

"Jennifer embraces the power of a quiet leaders and shows us how to empower ourselves as introverts to drive success. A quiet leader is often overlooked; this book has the tools and shows the path to visibility and empowerment as an introverted leader. Jennifer has turned her understanding of what an introverted leader is into a road map to success for the quiet leader."

—Diane Kelly, global security leader, Veralto

"As a chief people officer and a coach, I know how critical it is to honor the different ways people think, work, and lead. Jennifer Marcou brilliantly illuminates the strengths introverts bring to organizations and offers actionable tools to help them grow and have impact with confidence. *Lead with Quiet Confidence* is essential reading for anyone committed to developing their people authentically and unlocking the full potential of quiet, thoughtful talent."

—Ana White, EVP and chief people &
AI enablement officer, Lumen

"A very readable and practical guide for introverts based on the author's experience as a leader and a coach."

—Jennifer B. Kahnweiler, Ph.D., author
of *The Introverted Leader*

"Remarkable inventions often come from the quietest people in the loudest rooms. In *Lead with Quiet Confidence*, Jennifer Marcou ensures those ideas don't stay hidden—including yours."

—Tara Lemméy, inventor and founder of LENS, board member of the Ditchley Foundation and Weil Foundation

"Even though I consider myself an extrovert, I found this book a helpful guide to understanding how to be a better leader and supporter of those who are introverts. As well, there were so many helpful tips and I look forward to applying those in my own life. I wish I had read this book earlier in my career. Thank you Jennifer for sharing your wealth of experience and passion for leadership with others."

—Tara Roth, former corporate vice president of engineering, Microsoft

"I used to play 'follow the leader' as a child, mimicking whatever the leader did and then taking a stab at leading my own way. In *Lead with Quiet Confidence*, Jennifer Marcou shows how to embrace that concept in your career, guiding you to become a leader on your own terms. She acknowledges that introverts often face challenges in highly extroverted workplaces, emphasizing that it's not about trying to be something you're not. Instead, it's about paying attention to your environment and audience, adapting as needed while using your strengths.

As introvert leaders, we're constantly shifting gears—like patting our heads and rubbing our bellies at the same time. Marcou offers lots of encouragement and plenty of useful strategies for a daily practice of adapting, bringing forth what you need to solve problems, while ensuring everyone feels included and valued."

—Nancy Ancowitz, career strategist and author of *Self-Promotion for Introverts*

"In the many years I've known Jennifer Marcou, she's often made me wish I were an introvert. Her authenticity, thoughtful generosity, and leadership presence all flow from a dynamic inner life. As a gifted executive coach, she is unhurried, and I've noticed, appreciative of pauses that we both take. If you are an emerging introverted leader, this practical and inspiring book will help you to leverage your inner strengths, building both their voice and their visibility. Jennifer's LEAD framework reflects quintessential coaching."

—Patty Burgin, master certified coach,
author, founder and CEO at SeattleCoach

"Marcou's book reminds introverts of their differences, strengths, and vulnerabilities and provides strategies for embracing those differences, building on those strengths, and managing vulnerabilities so that they can move towards more self-assured power—a quiet confidence that can help (we) introverts to thrive, especially within the challenging environments of the workplace."

—Arnie Kozak, Ph.D., author
of *The Awakened Introvert*

". . . the qualities that get overlooked in extrovert-designed workplaces are the same qualities that make someone worth following. Deep thinking. Careful listening. The ability to read a room while everyone else is talking. . . . I particularly appreciated the attention to women introverts, who face the double bind of being culturally penalized for both quietness and assertiveness. Jennifer doesn't shy away from that reality. She names it and then hands the reader a way through. This book is a gift to anyone who has ever felt overlooked in a meeting, exhausted after a networking event, or quietly convinced that leadership wasn't built for someone like them."

—Annie Ricci, MA, LMFT, master certified coach

LEAD *with* QUIET CONFIDENCE

LEAD *with* QUIET CONFIDENCE

A Practical Guide *to* Success *for* Introverts

JENNIFER MARCOU

GREENLEAF
BOOK GROUP PRESS

Published by Greenleaf Book Group Press
Austin, Texas
www.gbgpress.com

Distributed by Greenleaf Book Group

For ordering information or special discounts for bulk purchases, please contact Greenleaf Book Group at PO Box 91869, Austin, TX 78709, 512.891.6100.

Design and composition by Greenleaf Book Group
Cover design by Greenleaf Book Group
Cover images used under license from ©Adobestock.com

Publisher's Cataloging-in-Publication data is available.

Print ISBN: 979-8-88645-529-8

eBook ISBN: 979-8-88645-530-4

To offset the number of trees consumed in the printing of our books, Greenleaf donates a portion of the proceeds from each printing to the Arbor Day Foundation. Greenleaf Book Group has replaced over 50,000 trees since 2007.

Printed in the United States of America on acid-free paper

26 27 28 29 30 31 32 33 10 9 8 7 6 5 4 3 2 1

First Edition

Contents

I dedicate this book to all the introverts whose leadership is ready to blossom.

And the day came when the risk to remain tight in a bud was more painful than the risk it took to blossom.

—Anaïs Nin

Introduction

Join the Quiet Awakening of Introverts

In a gentle way, you can shake the world.
—Mahatma Gandhi

Ten years ago, I cried in front of fifty other senior leaders, including my boss and mostly male colleagues.

I was not presenting, thank goodness. I was in a diversity training called "Dialogues Across Differences." Actors played out scenarios in which people felt excluded or stereotyped. In one scene, an introverted woman stated a point in a team meeting, but no one paid attention to her. Then another person, a man, made that same point and everyone acknowledged it.

The moderator, perhaps sensing this scenario was hitting close to home for me, stopped three feet in front of me and said, "Right at this point we will have a few people start to cry." And right on cue, tears started rolling down my cheeks. This scene epitomized my experience as an introvert at work, especially when I was more junior. *Why don't people hear me?*

At the time, I had worked at Microsoft, and before that American Express, for decades. I was a leader of leaders, managing thirty-plus people for years. But until that moment, I had not realized how much pain I carried and how hard it was to maintain my integrity as an introvert and rise through the leadership ranks. Countless times, I had tried to speak up, to be front and center and expend a lot of energy to be something I was not. Still, I had been overlooked or had my ideas misattributed to someone else. It was like I was invisible. It hurt.

It was not until that training that I realized all those times of not being heard had worn on me like sandpaper. After a career of not feeling heard, I was rubbed raw, had metaphoric scar tissue, and felt alone. Hence, the tears and raw emotion in that inopportune moment.

Having lived my life as an introvert, I know that we can feel insignificant—not because of our lack of capability or value but because our natural strengths and communication patterns are incompatible with systems designed to recognize and reward extroverted behaviors. We feel insignificant not because we are but because our significance is expressed in ways that often go overlooked, unappreciated, or underestimated in traditionally extroverted environments.

When I had experienced those feelings in the past, it was hard to imagine a world where I and other introverts could be our authentic quiet selves, be influential, and be leaders people follow. Over time, I became that quiet, influential leader. Now, that image is a vision I want to help make true for you.

The purpose of this book is to shift your mindset that the best leaders must be extroverted. I'm here to share the good news: You can become a quiet, confident, influential leader. Like me, your feelings of being ignored or somehow inadequate can change. You can find ways to speak up and reclaim your ideas. You can find ways to reenergize after long hours in meetings.

With this book, I want to help you find ways to approach your work that uniquely suit you as an introvert. It is about changing behaviors, as well as changing your mindset and building confidence.

Challenges Facing an Introverted Leader

As an undergraduate, I took an operations course. The students had to act out being leaders in a company. The teacher selected who was going to be the president in the executive team, and she did not select me, even though I did well in the class and knew I had the skills to do it. But I was a quiet one in the class. The more outspoken person, who happened to be a man, got to be president. That was my first lesson that being quiet (especially as a woman) was a barrier. Becoming a leader is not just about our capabilities; it's about how people *perceive* our capabilities.

Once I reached the corporate world, I saw again that being quiet was a detriment and that I wouldn't be recognized just for doing good work. I had to be visible. People listen to the ideas of those who speak up. And certain people spoke most of the time. I didn't want to interrupt them. I also didn't think my ideas were always valuable. But I quickly realized that if someone is speaking up it does not mean they're smarter than I am or have better ideas; it just means they speak up. Plus, we all know situations where there's someone who just can't shut up, whether or not they add value. I did not want to be one of those people. I didn't want to speak up unless I had something meaningful to contribute.

I also recognized that I had to exert energy to speak up, which meant that to align with the leadership ideal, I had to work differently than my natural mode so I could come up with ideas quickly in a meeting or follow up afterward. I had to manage my self-critical voice when I was doing very poorly what extroverts do naturally: speak on the spot, be engaging, even enjoy the happy hours.

Introversion Helped Me Succeed

It took a lot of years of experimentation, but I learned how to conquer the challenges facing introverted leaders. That training I mentioned in the beginning made me realize how far I had come. I had been promoted many times with larger remits and teams, eventually reaching vice president and general manager roles at American Express and Microsoft. I have managed hundreds of people. I have coached hundreds of people, the majority of them introverted.

Eventually, what I came to realize is that I was able to climb the corporate ladder to leadership levels not *despite* my introversion but *because* of my introversion. How can that be, when extroversion is usually seen as a required attribute for leadership?

I used my introverted strengths to listen to others, be thoughtful in making decisions, observe what others may not see, and leverage my calmness to lead my team through challenges of economic downturns, layoffs, and changes in regulations. I also used my powers to truly connect to people in authentic ways to empower the team and celebrate successes without the big fanfare. That's how I became a leader people followed, one who drove change and innovation in calm and rational ways and one who inspired others to be their authentic selves versus the traditional role model of extroverted leadership. Senior leaders could now see the quiet confidence I brought to the business and rewarded me with multiple promotions to more senior-level roles.

Most importantly, the lessons I learned demonstrated that I could succeed without changing *me*. As I'll talk about later in the book, there is brain science behind why introverts think and act differently from extroverts. We cannot change our fundamental biology even if we wanted to. We introverts, as individuals and as a community, need to be proud of who we are and stop acting like we're something we are not.

When we pretend that we're extroverts, it's exhausting. This book is about stopping that farce. It is about stopping being embarrassed to admit that you do not want to do anything with others on the weekend as you recharge your battery from all the work meetings. It's about seeing the introverted tendencies—like being thoughtful, observant, and good listeners—as distinct strengths. It's about being proud of being an introvert in an extroverted world.

> "When introverts fully embrace who we are, we undergo a kind of inner alchemy. We transform what society labels as negative traits into our greatest assets. Rather than trying to fix or cure our quieter qualities, we cultivate them . . . This inner alchemy process creates a kind of self-love that is unconditional."
>
> —Michaela Chung, *The Irresistible Introvert*

I did not change who I am. The many introverts I've coached have not changed who they are. Rather, we changed behaviors so that our strengths as introverts can shine. You, too, do not need to change who you are to be a successful leader. Be you. I am living proof you can still be introverted you and be a great leader.

YOU ARE NOT ALONE

I also wrote this book so you know you're not alone. Even though everyone is reading this book by themselves, we are in community, in our introverted way. One of the most powerful parts of my Lead with Quiet Confidence programs is that

continued

introverts connect with other introverts. It gives them confidence that someone understands them and is rooting for them. It gives them a community, their tribe. So let this book introduce you to your tribe and the learnings we can all share so we can pass on to others.

How This Book Can Help

The tear-filled training was also when I realized that I had something to share with other introverts. I had stuck it out and developed techniques that would work for me to be heard, for me to use my strengths as an introvert, and, most importantly, for me to accept and be fully proud of who I am and my work.

I wrote this book to help reduce the pain from being an introvert in a workplace that demands us to speak out loud. I want introverted people to be better prepared to deal with challenges that come with being quiet in an extroverted workplace. The techniques I have developed work. They have worked for me, and they have worked for my clients. They can work for you and save you years of being overlooked and underestimated.

And that is what this book is about. *It is not about turning you into an extrovert.* It is about celebrating who you are *and* incorporating new behaviors to make you even more successful.

When I started my coaching business in 2020, I wrote my vision as a coach:

A world where the quiet lead

My passion is serving accomplished, impact-driven introverts to increase their confidence and have greater impact at work, without changing who they are. I want to help them lead with quiet confidence.

This book is structured to provide the fundamentals of what will help you gain the courage and insight to be successful being you. The book follows the framework of the Lead with Quiet Confidence® Bridge, starting from insignificance and moving to impact through the three phases, Awareness, Confidence, and Behaviors.

Figure 0.1: The Lead with Quiet Confidence Bridge

There are four parts of the book:

- **Part I: Awareness—What Do I Need to Know to Be Successful as an Introvert?** The three chapters of this section will debunk the negative associations of introverted leadership, help you recognize how your brain operates differently, and provide insights into how your strengths can be leveraged effectively. It introduces what I call the LEAD with Quiet Confidence Framework, which is an action model that will help you turn aspirations into accomplishments.
- **Part II: Confidence—How to Build and Exude Confidence:** The four chapters here demonstrate that confidence is teachable, not unreachable, with various frameworks and exercises.
- **Part III: Behaviors—Practical Guide to Being Successful as a Leader:** The five chapters in this section describe specific strategies you can use to succeed as an introverted leader by changing behaviors, not who you are. You can experiment with behaviors

and do one thing out of your comfort zone to drive the impact you want. For example, you will learn to speak up and voice your ideas—just say it. Or share your accomplishments with your boss and colleagues to be more visible—just send that email. Or you will learn to show up as your authentic self in networking situations. By the end of this section, you will learn to "say it, send it, show up."

- **Part IV: Impact—Turning Insight into Implementation:** The chapters in this part will help guide you in developing an action plan.

Each chapter ends with Actions to Consider to help you implement the ideas from that chapter if you decide it's an area you want or need to work on. I don't expect or even want you to think you need to act on all the ideas in this book. Rather, I want to provide you options in hopes you find one thing (or maybe a few things!) that you can do to make progress toward a professional or personal goal. My clients and I are living proof that having more impact, success, confidence, growth, and happiness while staying your authentic self is possible! You have to take the first step to make it possible for you.

I've liberally sprinkled stories throughout the book inspired by both my life as an introvert and the experiences of my coaching clients who have experienced challenges with leadership as an introvert. My hope is that you will see yourself in my and my client's stories and can learn from our shared experiences as introverts. In all cases, I have changed identifying details to keep their identities anonymous. I would love to hear your stories, too.

Everyone will have their own journey. I am excited to be on that journey with you. I thank you for allowing me to be alongside you in your personal journey of development so you, too, can lead with quiet confidence.

This book is based on my thirty years of corporate leadership experience and a decade of coaching hundreds of introverts. It was written for you with love, and I hope you feel it. But mostly, I hope you find that love for yourself.

ACTION WORKBOOK

I've written this book for introverts who want to take action to leverage their introvert strengths to achieve a personal or professional goal. To help you toward that goal, please download the *Lead with Quiet Confidence Workbook* to work through the exercises in this book at www.JenniferMarcou.com/resources.

PART I

AWARENESS:
What Do I Need to Know to Be Successful as an Introvert?

Part I of this book will explain the history and biology of introversion, which will provide a framework for later chapters about how to build confidence and success as an introvert. First we will cover facts about introversion, studying some famous and not-so-famous introverts. Then you'll learn about the introverted brain and how introverts are biologically different from extroverts and the strengths we bring to the party. Finally, I'll introduce the LEAD framework, which is a model you can apply to make the changes you want to make and achieve the goals you want to achieve, leading with your introverted strengths and quiet confidence.

1

Introversion and Quiet Confidence

Our culture is biased against quiet and
reserved people, but introverts are responsible
for some of humanity's greatest achievements.
—Susan Cain

When I ask people who are clearly introverts if they are an introvert, they quickly say something along the lines of, "Oh no, I'm not an introvert. I have friends."

Why are people embarrassed about being labeled an introvert? Why does introversion have a bad reputation? How can we reclaim the power of introversion? How can we be proud to be an introvert who leads with quiet confidence? Those are the questions I'll address in this chapter.

The Awakening of an Introvert

I first officially learned that I am an introvert when I took a Myers-Briggs test at my first job after business school. I had known all my life I was quiet. As an only child, I was perfectly content to play by myself. I used to "play school" with my stuffed animals—with Truffles the big white polar bear as the teacher. In grade school, I was not lonely being a latch-key kid coming home from school to an empty house. I don't remember being bored. Rather, I loved the quiet time and doing what I wanted to do—have a snack, play piano, ride my bike, organize my books. But until I took the Myers-Briggs test, I didn't call myself an introvert.

During one off-site related to the Myers-Briggs test, we participants organized ourselves into introverted and extroverted groups. In our introverted group, we identified questions we would pose to our extroverted colleagues. I remember there was this energy and excitement to ask questions that were actually quite demeaning. *Why do you talk so much? Why do you interrupt me? Why can't you shut up?*

And from the other side of the room, the extroverts strangely and ironically asked more thoughtful questions. *Why are you so quiet? What can help you speak up more?*

I realized that we introverts had a lot of anger toward extroverts, having to pretend to be like them. When the extroverts recognized our differences, they got really curious. Over time, I realized that anger was neither healthy nor productive.

Then at some point, I took another assessment, the Team Management Profile. Compared to my group, I was at the extreme end of introversion. In fact, I was more introverted than 97 percent of every person who'd ever taken that test. My colleagues were surprised. I didn't seem like an introvert to them, because I interacted collaboratively and engagingly with people. But I was proud! The label represented who I was and what I felt. I preferred working by myself or in small groups versus larger groups. I was very thoughtful and prepared in advance for discussions, as I hated speaking on the spot. I did not like to rush to decisions but preferred to weigh all the angles. I could concentrate for long periods of time and looked at things very analytically. I was exhausted by all-day meetings and off-sites and hated evening work events. I knew I needed to reenergize after energy-draining activities with lots of people or stimulation. I just liked my independence and autonomy to do what I wanted.

Later in my career, I took yet another personality test that again showed my strong introversion. My husband read my profile and asked why I would want my colleagues, and especially my boss, to see it. Wouldn't I be embarrassed? Isn't a leader supposed to be more outgoing? I responded, "I am what I am." By that point, I was already successfully leading a team of twenty, so I was not trying to prove I could be a leader; I already was one, even if I was quiet, calm, and thoughtful but not gregarious.

Before diving further into the idea that introversion can be a strength, let's first get our definitions aligned.

What Is Introversion?

Introversion is a personality trait and a tendency to be focused predominantly on internal thoughts and feelings rather than on external things or social interaction. Myers-Briggs defines *introversion* and *extroversion* as preferences, as shown in Table 1.1.

Preferences of Introverts	Preferences of Extroverts
• Think before acting • Spend time in reflection • Think things through • Be contained, gain energy from concentration • Have a depth of interests	• Act before thinking • Act quickly • Talk things through • Be expressive • Gain energy from interaction • Have a breadth of interests

Table 1.1: Myers-Briggs descriptions of introverts and extroverts

Other attributes that Myers-Briggs notes include the notion that introverts tend to enjoy quiet and solitary activities, such as reading, writing, or meditating. They can participate in social activities but may feel drained and need time alone to recharge their energy. Introverts tend to be more in their heads, while extroverts tend to be more impacted by their external environment.

While all of that is true, I prefer the much simpler definition from Susan Cain, author of *Quiet: The Power of Introverts in a World That Can't Stop Talking*, who explains the distinction this way:

- **Introverts** get energy from **being by themselves**.
- **Extroverts** get energy from **being with others**.

Of course, there is a spectrum. There are no pure introverts. We all have some extroverted thoughts or behaviors in certain situations. So, in truth, we are all really ambiverts—in between introverts and extroverts. Still, there are preferences toward one side or the other. Even within introverts there are many different types of introverts—no two are alike. One introvert might be very quiet, while another might have no problem expressing themselves but be exhausted at the end of a day of all-day meetings. In this book, I will refer to introverts as binary to extroverts, but always remember that there is a spectrum. When I say *introvert*, I will be referring to introverted preferences in generalities. Not everything will resonate with how you show up. Take in what resonates with you. I recognize that we can all be ambiverts and can shift behaviors in certain situations and certainly learn behaviors over time.

Another important understanding of the introversion-extroversion spectrum is that it is a temperament you are born with. As Jenn Granneman, author of *The Secret Lives of Introverts*, states, "Temperament refers to your inborn traits that organize how you approach the world, while personality can be defined as the pattern of behavior, thoughts, and emotions that make you an individual. It can take years to build a personality, but your temperament is something you are born with."

INTROVERSION IS NOT SHYNESS

Introversion sometimes gets confused with shyness. People who are shy fear social interactions and negative judgment. Introverts, on the other hand, don't fear social interactions. They are drained by them and see chitchatting as especially useless, as they prefer deeper, more meaningful conversations. Shyness and introversion can overlap, but there are shy extroverts and not-shy introverts.

Why Does Introversion Have a Bad Reputation?

We live in a society that is biased toward extroversion. This is no more evident than in two common personality tests for introversion: the HEXACO Personality Inventory and the Big Five. The heart of both tests is a measurement of the degree of extroversion, whether it is strongly present or notably absent. The implied message of these tests is that, by default, we introverts are failed extroverts.

For example, when you review the six facets of extroversion as defined by the HEXACO Personality Inventory, you find the definition of introversion is the opposite of extroversion, which are not always positive definitions:

- **Friendliness**—the low-scoring introverted description is "**distant or reserved**."
- **Gregariousness**—the low-scoring introverted description is "**socially withdrawn**."

- **Assertiveness**—the low-scoring introverted description is "**not talking much** and **letting others control** the activities of groups."
- **Activity level**—the low-scoring introverted description is "**slower**, more leisurely, relaxed pace."
- **Excitement-seeking**—the low-scoring introverted description is "**overwhelmed by noise and commotion** and **adverse to thrill-seeking**."
- **Cheerfulness**—the low-scoring introverted description is "**not prone to such energetic, high spirits**."

Do you want to be described as a "distant, socially withdrawn, letting others control, slower, overwhelmed, not prone to high spirits" person? Would you want to hire someone with that description? Or would you rather hire a "friendly, gregarious, assertive, energetic, risk-taking, cheerful" person, as would describe an extrovert?

This demonstrates the problem with the standard measurement for introversion and the misconceived perceptions of what introverts are and the unique gifts they offer and illustrates why people are hesitant to admit they are introverts. It feels like something is wrong with us. The Western world revolves around extroverts—from our school systems, which value class participation, to work, where you must speak up in meetings and give presentations, to our social lives, where we are expected to go to and enjoy parties even if we don't want to.

I once asked a group of introverts in my Lead with Quiet Confidence program to describe the consequences they'd felt in their careers as a result of being introverted. Their answers are summarized in Table 1.2, and you can see there are a lot of negatives and challenges that come with introversion.

How Introversion Negatively Impacts My Career	
People who speak up get noticed, get more respect, have more visibility, and get promoted.	People talk over introverts.
Introverts get passed over for promotions.	No natural opening to speak for introverts
Introverts need to self-promote, which is uncomfortable.	Introverts are surrounded by louder people.
Work requires quick thinking, and that does not fit with introverts' preference for and strength of deep thinking.	People are rewarded for speaking up, which is harder for an introvert.
Perception of lack of leadership	Lots of meetings are exhausting to an introvert.
Perception that introverts don't care, don't have an opinion, and can't influence others	Events/social hours are stressful, energy depleting, and feel like an obligation.

Table 1.2: Career consequences of being an introvert

When society reinforces these negative stereotypes of introverts, we tell ourselves that there is something wrong with us. We feel the need to change and force ourselves to be gregarious, energetic extroverts.

Wrong!

It is time to stand up and change the story for introverts.

ARE EXTROVERTS HAPPIER?

Another knock against introversion is the perception that extroverts are happier than introverts, perhaps because they are more energetic, agreeable, or willing to take risks. But research from Peter Hills and Michael Argyle indicates that life regard (the identification of meaning and purpose in life), self-esteem, life orientation (the level of optimism and pessimism), and mental stability are much more important to happiness than introversion or extroversion. In other words, significance and

continued

connection are bigger drivers of happiness than extroversion. There are happy introverts and unhappy introverts, just like there are happy extroverts and unhappy extroverts.

Perceptions and Challenges of Introversion

The group of introverts I mentioned above also identified these introvert descriptors:

- **Quiet**—reserved, not outgoing, shy, wallflower, aloof, demure
- **Introspective**—thinker, thoughtful, reflective
- **Energy management**—derive energy from quiet time, space, and being with themselves, need alone time, drive for anonymity, reserved in their energy
- **Listener and observer**—observational, active listener and observer

Notice how some of these qualities, such as *active listener* and *thoughtful*, are strengths, while others, like *shy*, *wallflower*, *aloof*, and *need time alone* could be interpreted negatively. Even *quiet* and r*eserved* could be seen as negative if the standard or culture is to be more outgoing.

These attributes, combined with the negative associations shown in Table 1.2, make life as an introvert challenging. Jennifer B. Kahnweiler, author of *The Introverted Leader* and *Quiet Influence*, identifies the following challenges for introverts in the workplace:

- People exhaustion
- Needing to make quick decisions in fast-paced environments
- Getting interrupted
- Pressure to self-promote
- Emphasis on working in teams

Based on my own experiences and those of countless other introverts I've talked with, I'd add two more challenges for introverts to that list:

- Lowered privacy boundaries
- Pressure to act extroverted

Introverts can be amazing leaders. Spoiler alert—Bill Gates, Oprah Winfrey, and Abraham Lincoln are introverts. How can we turn around our perception and the world's perception to focus on the strengths, even the *superpowers*, of introverts?

Building Quiet Confidence as an Introvert

If introverts have so many challenges, both in preferences impacting their careers and in reputation, can introverts be strong leaders? When asked to identify the superpowers of introverts, those in the Lead with Quiet Confidence program provided the answers shown in Table 1.3.

Thoughtfulness and Reflection	**Listening Skills**
Thoughtful	Good listener
Analytical	Perceptive
Problem-solver	Empathetic
See the bigger picture	Calm
Deliberate	Less emotional
Focus and Concentration	**Self-Awareness**
High concentration	Self-reflective
Detail oriented	Independent
Task oriented	In tune with their energy
Prepared	
Accountable	

Table 1.3: Leadership-useful attributes of an introvert

I don't know about you, but I think this list shows a lot of desirable traits for a leader. According to *Forbes*, a leader has "the ability to inspire, influence and guide others toward a common goal or vision. A leader positively affects others purely by who they are and how they act in a group environment . . . Anyone can exhibit leadership qualities regardless of their job title or position." I think these introvert attributes are consistent with that definition (and is why I think we introverts should always refer to ourselves as leaders regardless of our title, our level, or whether we manage people).

Can Quiet Introverts Be Strong Leaders?

Researchers Deniz Ones and Stephan Dilchert found that top executives score higher in extroversion in the Big Five personality test than do people at any lower leadership levels. Put another way, the percentage of introverts decreases the higher you go in the corporate ladder. For example, *The Wall Street Journal* developed data showing that while 50 percent of the general population is introverted, only 12 percent of supervisors and 2 percent of the very top executives are below average in extroversion (i.e., are considered introverted), as shown in Figure 1.1. Surely, if 50 percent of the population is introverted (or "below average for extroversion"), there is room for more introverts in these top echelons, and in leadership positions at all levels.

While the exact figures from *The WSJ* may be debatable, there does seem to be a consistent view that there is a very small percentage of leaders who are introverts. You've likely perceived from your own experience that leaders are typically extroverted. We do live in a world, particularly in the US, where extroversion is the ideal for leaders. *The Hustle* website reports that "some 65 percent of senior executives see introversion as a 'barrier to leadership,' and only 6 percent think introverts have the people skills required to oversee a successful team."

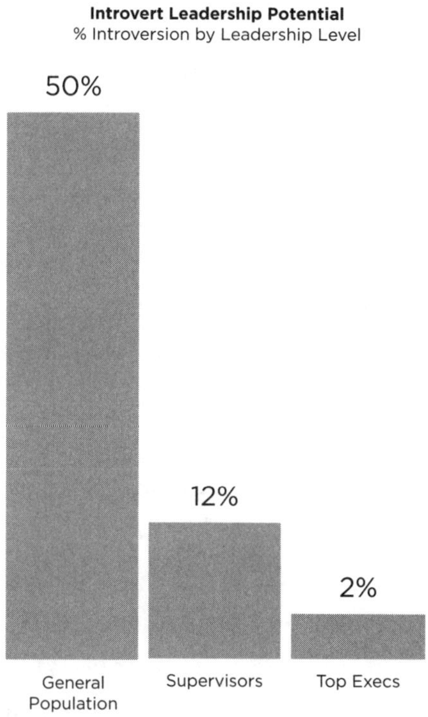

Figure 1.1: Percentage of introverts decreases the higher the leadership level.

Remember, approximately half of the population is considered introverted. About half the leaders should be introverts. How can we increase the percentage of introverted leaders?

Despite the fact that the work world is set up for extroverts, I am sure you can name several leaders who you personally know and famous leaders who are introverts. Let's look at some famous introverts who prove introverts can, in fact, be great leaders. There are probably a few names on this list that surprise you: Oprah Winfrey, Ruth Bader Ginsberg, Meryl Streep, Shonda Rhimes, Rosa Parks, Amy Schumer, Albert Einstein, Abraham Lincoln, FDR, Eleanor Roosevelt, Steven Spielberg, Mahatma Gandhi, Marissa Mayer, Warren Buffett, and Bill Gates.

Some of these leaders have stated they are introverts. Other historical figures have been surmised to be introverted from their characteristics or behaviors, such as seeking time alone, deep reflection, strong listening or observational skills, or their direct quotes about such preferences.

Abraham Lincoln once said, "I am rather inclined to silence."

Warren Buffett said, "I insist on a lot of time being spent, almost every day, to just sit and think."

Oprah Winfrey stated, "Alone time is when I distance myself from the voices of the world so I can hear my own."

Albert Einstein said, "The monotony and solitude of a quiet life stimulates the creative mind."

Eleanor Roosevelt stated, "I wonder if anyone else glories in cold and snow without, an open fire within, and the luxury of a tray of food all by one's self in one's own room? I realize it sounds extremely selfish and a little off to look upon this as a festive occasion. Nevertheless, last night was a festive occasion for I spent it in this way."

The leaders above and other introverts have many of the quiet strengths that *Forbes* and *The Introvert Blog* identify as being useful for leaders:

- Reflective
- Thoughtful decision-making
- Strong critical thinking and problem-solving abilities
- Strong listening skills
- Calm under pressure
- Leading through empathy, accepting and inclusive
- Putting others first
- Building effective teams
- Utilizing solitude as a strength
- Humility
- Ability to adapt their style based on what is needed

That last point—being able to adapt their style—is critical for each person's success. Steven Spielberg would not have been a successful director if he did not have the ability to put himself out there to sell himself to influence movie studios to invest in his ideas and to convince actors to join his movies. Bill Gates would not have been able to build Microsoft as founder and CEO without taking a risk and making quick decisions when he promised Microsoft's first customer a yet-undeveloped product. People in the limelight, like Oprah Winfrey, Meryl Streep, and Amy Schumer, have to be in the public eye even though their preference may be to curl up on a couch at home with a good book. And even the more cerebral types like Albert Einstein had to convince the world of their ideas when they may have preferred time alone to think more deeply about their ideas. All these introverts leveraged their strengths as an introvert and, at the same time, adapted behaviors to be successful and have impact in the world. Introverts can be leaders by changing their behaviors, not who they are.

INTROVERTS CAN BE LEADERS BY CHANGING THEIR BEHAVIORS, NOT WHO THEY ARE.

Consider the strengths of an introvert and how they complement the requirements to be a leader. For example, leaders need quiet time to reflect and think; introverts do this naturally. Leaders need to be calm and considered; introverts are built that way. Leaders need to be observant and good problem-solvers; introverts excel at this. Researchers Adam Grant, Francesca Gino, and David Hoffman found that, in certain situations, introverts can actually be better leaders. For instance, introverts excel at leading a team of people who contribute ideas and are proactive, whereas extroverts are better at leading a team of people who want to be told what to do. Depending on the company or team goals, the extroverted leadership ideal is not always the best fit.

I love the story of Mahatma Gandhi. Widely regarded for his nonviolent resistance against British rule in India, Gandhi inspired civil rights and freedom movements all over the globe. As a child, he would run home from school every day so he would not have to talk to anyone, yet as an adult, he used those same introverted tendencies to lead the movement for India's independence through his introverted civil disobedience. He started with his deep contemplation of justice and development of his philosophy of nonviolence. His singular actions such as a hunger strike had a profound impact on the world, shaking it to awareness of the injustices of the British electoral decisions. His planned days of silence became a powerful tool, allowing him to focus on his message around social justice and communicate it in written form—no one could talk over him in writing. He leveraged his strengths as an introvert and focused on his passion to take action. He certainly changed behaviors from running away to avoid talking to people to sharing his perspective without changing the core of who he was. As he once said, "In a gentle way, you can shake the world."

Introverts as Accomplished Leaders

Introverts can be leaders by changing their behaviors, not who they are. You, too, can be the authentic—and introverted—leader you want to be and build on your quiet strengths. Take my client Nandy, for example. Here's her story:

> Nandy said that for years she'd forced herself to go to parties and join study groups in college even though she didn't want to, since that was what she thought was required to be socially accepted. As she started her career in financial services and rose to the vice president level, she was more outgoing when she needed to be in

work situations. But it was exhausting being more outgoing in meetings, speaking her opinion. She would have to find time alone to read on the couch in the evenings to reenergize.

Nandy continues to build her confidence in her introvert skills and practice behaviors that allow her to engage in an extrovert-oriented world. How did she overcome the challenges to being her authentic self? First, she identified her natural inclinations and the impact on the perceptions of her colleagues. Then she identified where she wanted to change her behaviors to be more successful at work. Then she found a way to meld those new behaviors in a natural way with her introverted preferences and strengths instead of "acting" like an extrovert.

Now Nandy runs her own consulting business and changes her behaviors as the business needs, while still staying her authentic self by spending time alone in deep thought about the strategy of her business. That enables her to be more socially interactive when she is selling her services to potential clients. She no longer tries to be something else but uses different tools or behaviors in her toolbox to meet the needs of the situation.

Embrace Your Introversion!

We have addressed the definition of introversion as getting energy from being alone versus being with people. Introverts can be perfectly fine socializing but need quiet time to recharge. We also discussed the bias against introversion in standard personality tests. And we certainly see that bias in our day-to-day world, with the constant need to be out in front and the expectation to engage socially and on social media. There are some perceived and real challenges introverts face that can negatively impact our careers if we don't do something about it.

But "doing something about it" does not mean turning into or acting like an extrovert. Rather, it is about defining the leader you want to be, with all your introverted tendencies, your superpowers as an introvert, your passions and your values. Think of the times you excel at speaking up and leverage those abilities to change your behavior in other situations. There are many stories of introverts who were successful by just being themselves.

To reiterate a key message, this book is not about turning you into an extrovert; it is about adapting some behaviors, so you can be the successful and authentic leader you want to be.

In my own journey as an introvert, I went from knowing I was different as a child and challenged at work situations, to learning the term *introvert*, to learning skills to be a leader despite being an introvert, to now being so confident in my own skin I can help other introverts shine. Just today, someone was surprised to hear I am an introvert. She said, "Oh, you are one of those polished introverts." I hope this book helps you find the polish you need to let your underlying strengths shine.

ACTIONS TO CONSIDER

If you feel inspired to take action based on this chapter, here are some ideas to get you started.

First, think about how you perceive your own introversion:

- Do you tell people you are an introvert? Why or why not? How do you tell them?
- Are you proud to be an introvert (or have introverted tendencies)? What are you proud of? What are you not proud of? What would you change if you could?

Second, as a way to frame what you can take away from the rest of this book, think about what kind of leader you want to be. Is there a quiet, introverted leader whose confidence you admire? What are the leadership attributes you admire about that person? What do you want to replicate in your own leadership?

Creating the vision of who you want to be is a foundation for the rest of the book. This will feed into your goals for Chapter 3.

I recommend doing some journaling about these prompts as a way to focus your thoughts and get clear on your goals. If it helps, download the *Lead with Quiet Confidence Workbook* at www.JenniferMarcou.com/resources.

2

Appreciating the Brilliance of Your Introvert Brain

Quiet people have the loudest minds.
—Stephen Hawking

Have you, an introvert, ever been in a meeting and felt like your brain was slow? Have you observed everyone else throwing out ideas, but your brain doesn't think of an idea until after the meeting? That has happened to me countless times. How frustrating! I beat myself up, asking myself, *Why can't my mind think faster?* This is quite common with introverts. Why? Because the introverted brain is different from the extroverted brain, causing differences in behaviors and preferences. As a result, this phenomenon of feeling like we can't come up with ideas is actually quite normal for us introverts.

But, as we've already seen, introverted differences aren't weaknesses; they can be wielded for strength. In this chapter, I will explore the biological reasons why introvert and extrovert brains operate differently and show how understanding the science helps shift the narrative around who introverts are.

Biological Differences and Reframing Perceptions

There are biological reasons that explain how your brain operates. If you are like me, you may relish in learning about the science of the brain, neurotransmitters, and their impact on how introvert brains operate. If science is not your thing, it is not important to learn all the details of why the introvert brain is different; rather, my hope is that understanding the biology behind introversion will show why it's fruitless to try to change our fundamental introvert nature. The point is to learn the strengths and challenges the biological factors create and focus on leveraging our strengths and mitigating the challenges.

Let's look at five negative perceptions about introverts, the brain science behind those perceptions, and how we can reframe the narrative into positive messages.

1. "Slow Thinker" Becomes "Deep-Thinking Advantage"

The longer time it takes for an introvert to come up with an idea is based in biology. Introverts have a thicker prefrontal cortex, the tissue responsible for deep thought, planning, analysis, focus, introspection, and decision-making. (See Figure 2.1.) This extra thickness arises because we have more neurons and nerve fibers in the gray and white matter—meaning there are more connections between neurons, allowing for more links between ideas. Extroverts, on the other hand, have a thinner prefrontal cortex. Their brains process information more quickly, less deeply, and they act more impulsively.

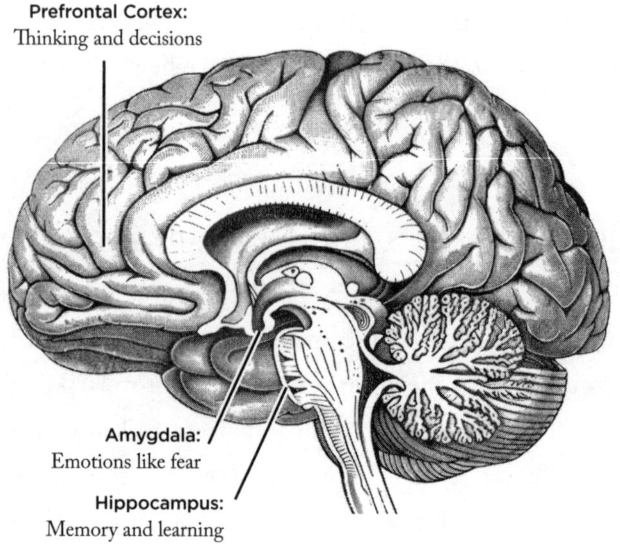

Figure 2.1: Differences in the prefrontal cortex give introverts a deep-thinking advantage.

According to *The Irresistible Introvert* author Michaela Chung, "One of the reasons it takes us longer to verbalize our thoughts is that introverts rely on long-term memory more than working memory. Accessing the right words from long-term memory takes longer."

This conclusion is supported by the work of Dr. Debra Johnson from the University of Iowa, who found that thoughts in an introvert's brain travel along different neurological pathways than extroverts. "An introvert's pathway is longer, more complex and internally focused. An extrovert's pathway is shorter, more straightforward and externally focused. Extroverts rely on short-term memory, the here and now. Introverts draw more from long-term memory taking into consideration the past, present and future."

The research of Dr. Robert Stelmack of the University of Ottawa reached a different conclusion about the reasons why introverts may be perceived as slow thinkers. His research found that introverts and extroverts may process information in the same amount of time, but it takes longer for introverts to take action, such as verbalizing their conclusions. In other words, it may seem that extroverts are processing faster, but in reality, both extroverts and introverts are thinking at the same speed. However, introverts are spending more time moving from thinking to verbalizing.

The message is that it takes longer for we introverts to share ideas or responses, which is challenging in a situation that requires us to respond quickly. To account for this, I recommend asking questions to allow your brain and voice time to catch up with your thoughts. Also, asking questions shows more engagement even if you are not yet sharing your ideas.

CHANGING THE "SLOW THINKING" NARRATIVE

Our thoughts take a longer path, and we take longer to verbalize thoughts. It's a myth that we are "slow thinkers." The better way to frame this phenomenon is "introverts have a deep-thinking advantage."

2. "Internal Focus" Becomes the "Observer's Edge"

We introverts have a reputation for being silent in meetings or social gatherings. That has been true for me.

But the external silence does not mean our brains are quiet. Quite the contrary: Introverts not only have thicker prefrontal cortexes, but they also have more blood flow to the prefrontal cortex, according to D. L. Johnson et al. from the *American Journal of Psychiatry*. There is more active thinking or taking in observations compared to extroverts. Yes, introverts are more introspective. They do more thinking than extroverts.

This internal thinking is not just ruminating about ourselves or our problems. The introverted brain takes in a lot more data from *observing* the outside world. Introverts are keen observers. Extroverts have more blood flow to *interpreting* sensory (external) data and less to the behavioral inhibition areas. Extroverts enjoy responding to external stimuli without inhibition because they are not "in their head" like introverts. Introverts, on the other hand, are absorbing all the external data and thinking through it before they respond. Introverts are more thoughtful and observant, and extroverts are more social, risk-taking, and externally focused.

In any meeting where I, as an introvert, am quiet, I am actually observing the dynamics of the room. I observe body language and hear tone to assess who likes an idea or not without them even voicing it. My observations can be extremely useful, especially when paired with an extrovert's perspective. For example, I once had a highly extroverted boss and in meetings, she would speak most of the time, while I would be observing the minute movements of everyone's facial expressions. I walked out with insight into what everyone thought, and she totally missed it, as she was talking the whole time. I would then share my observations, and we would create a plan for me to follow up one-on-one with those who were not yet on board with the plan. We were a highly complementary team—she was the megaphone, and I was the whisperer. We influenced a lot more people together than individually.

CHANGING THE "INTERNAL FOCUS" NARRATIVE

Let's change the view that "introverts dwell only on the inside and have nothing to say" to "introverts have the observer's edge." An introvert being quiet does not mean they are not thinking. There is a lot going on in the introverted mind, from internal analysis to observing the outside world. An introvert is a wealth of knowledge if we as introverts can share more of our thinking externally to have impact.

3. "Loner" Becomes "Strategic Energy Management"

In contrast to popular tropes, introverts have the ability to build relationships and socialize with others, just like extroverts. The difference is that the introvert's energy gets depleted with too much social engagement, so an introvert needs time to replenish their energy. According to Dr. Marti Olsen Laney in her book *The Introvert Advantage*, the explanation can be found in an understanding of how dopamine (a neurotransmitter connected to rewards) operates in introverted versus extroverted brains:

- **Introverted brains are more sensitive to dopamine.** Too much dopamine can cause introverts to feel overstimulated and need to reduce stimulation to reenergize.
- **Extroverted brains have lower sensitivity to dopamine**, so they actually require a lot more of it. And they get more dopamine by interacting with others and taking action on the spot. Biologically speaking, they are more driven by socializing with others than introverts.

Given this difference, is it any wonder that introverts look like loners in comparison to extroverts?

Another factor at play here is introverts also have a higher base level of activation in their brains than extroverts. It is easier for introverts to get overstimulated in social or noisy situations. (See Figure 2.2.) Add on the perceived need to pretend to be an extrovert and work can be exhausting.

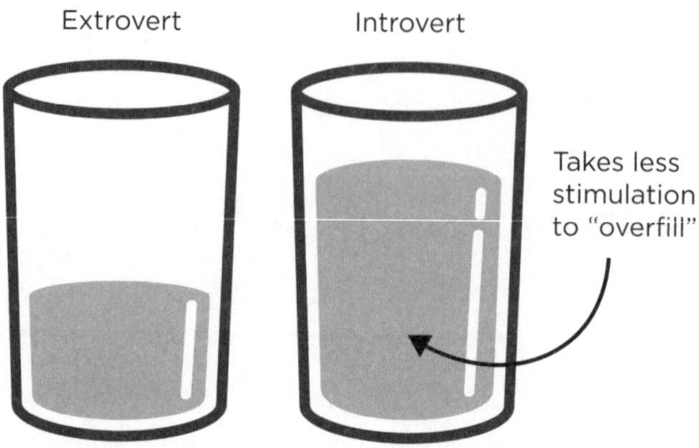

Figure 2.2: Introverts have a higher base level of brain activation.

This claim is backed up by a 1963 study by Hans Eysenck published in *Nature*, which found that introverts have higher arousal in the brain cortex than extroverts by showing that introverts create more saliva than extroverts when lemon juice is placed on their tongue. This indicates that introverts are more alert to stimulation and to cortisol, a stress-related hormone. Introverts "really do not need much stimulation to push them beyond the threshold of relaxation and into the realm of anxiety and overstimulation. Extroverts, however, have a lower starting point for arousal and therefore need more stimulation to get to the same point." With the same stimulus, the introverted brain will be at a higher level of arousal and is more likely to be overstimulated than the extroverted brain. In fact, introverts are also more sensitive to caffeine due to an already high level of arousal compared to extroverts.

Add the brain chemistry to the idea that introverts are constantly observing, analyzing, judging, and ruminating, and it shouldn't come as a surprise that socializing for introverts increases our cognitive load. Extroverts, in contrast, take the external environment at face value. Therefore, social engagements are more tiring for introverts, especially small talk.

The great news is there is a solution. Introverts can be aware of their energy patterns and what is overstimulating. Later in the book (especially Chapters 11 and 12), I'll explore techniques that introverts can use to manage their energy. Here are two examples:

- Plan our days to balance the overstimulation with energy-generating "activities" or just solitude.
- Direct "chitchatty" conversations to topics we care about. That is, we shouldn't get caught talking about the weather—unless we are really interested in the weather. Meaningless conversations are even more draining to an introvert.

CHANGING THE "LONER" NARRATIVE

Let's change the view that "introverts are not social" to "introverts can be social as long as they strategically manage their energy." Introverts can be connectors when they are mindful.

4. From "Risk Averse" to "Methodical Planner"

The brain differences described earlier reinforce the idea that introverts do a lot of thinking. Diving a bit deeper, sciences shows us that key parts of the introverted brain have a higher concentration of a neurotransmitter called glutamate, which is associated with learning and memory. In fact, it is most present in areas of the brain associated with memory, attention, planning, working memory, cognitive flexibility, problem-solving, and executive functions such as abstract reasoning and inhibition.

Unfortunately, high levels of glutamate can contribute to higher levels of anxiety, which is perhaps why we introverts are methodical planners. We tend to think through all the potential risks and what could go wrong and plan accordingly as a way to limit our anxiety. This insight also helps us understand why we introverts usually have good control of our impulses.

Admittedly, in some cases, this risk aversion can go to the extreme and result in an introvert not trying new things. But if you are aware of the need to try new things as a way to inspire new ideas, meet new people, and grow, this extreme risk aversion can be mitigated.

In contrast, extroverts have less concentration of glutamate in this brain region. They do not have as much control over their inhibitions and are willing to take more risks. They can seem more outgoing and out there and perhaps look like they are having more fun.

CHANGING THE "RISK AVERSE" NARRATIVE

Let's not focus on the risk aversion of introverts; let's focus on the correlating strength of methodical planning. While we may have to learn to push through our risk aversion, we can take credit for a strength in planning.

5. From "Antisocial Party Pooper" to "Powerfully Quiet"

Building on the myth that introverts can't be social, people also tend to think introverts are party poopers. Because we may be more risk averse and need quiet time to reenergize, it is more likely we will turn down offers to go for after-work drinks or will want to leave a party before it ends.

This feeling is biological. It is a preference driven by our brain chemistry. While extroverted brains are tied more to dopamine, the neurotransmitter of rewards, introverts have more blood flow to acetylcholine pathways.

Acetylcholine is a neurotransmitter that is connected to increased attention, staying calm, energy conservation, memory, and sense of well-being. Acetylcholine makes you feel good when you are calm or engaged in mentally challenging activities. Introverts recharge alone or with quiet activities to get more acetylcholine reward (whereas extroverts are rewarded by socializing), according to Christine Fonseca in *Quiet Kids*. So of course, an introvert is likely to seek out more quiet time. Acetylcholine also plays a role in the "slow thinking" narrative I discussed previously because its processing uses a longer pathway to generate feelings of pleasure than does the dopamine pathway. Extroverts' brains prefer the quick hit of a reward instead of the slower-acting reward, so extroverts are less comfortable with reduced stimuli.

Introverts are guided more by the parasympathetic nervous system, which is the "rest and digest" or throttle-down nervous system. In contrast, extroverts prefer the sympathetic nervous system, the more action-oriented system. This correlates with the introvert's need for more time without stimulus.

Quiet time is needed for all brains to come up with new ideas, make new connections in ideas, reenergize to better perform, reduce stress, and more. Introverts in particular are designed to reap the benefits of quiet if they allow themselves the luxury of occasional solitude despite living in a "together is better" culture. Introverts can be very aware of their environment, which enables them to notice details or patterns others do not, which in turn allows them to do a better job of identifying risks and threats and preparing to support creativity, strategic planning, and decision-making. Extroverts can even learn from introverts how to harness quiet time so they can be and perform at their best.

I have coached many introverts on how to deal with the requests for after-work drinks or dinner or the all-day meetings. When these draining events are important to attend for your job, that just means you need to plan for before, after, and throughout the event to regain a little more energy, such as going for a short walk alone or even resorting to seeking a few minutes of alone time in the bathroom. We will discuss more creative ways to find quiet in Chapter 12.

CHANGING THE "PARTY POOPER" NARRATIVE

Let's change the perception that "introverts are party poopers" to "introverts relish and harness the power of quiet." Introverts, give yourself grace if you want to say no to a party or want to leave early. All you extroverts, give the introverts a break when they want to find quiet time after social engagements or if they decline your invite even if they have "nothing else to do." Reading a book, sitting and thinking alone, or chilling out are not "nothing"—they are reenergizing for an introvert. And that quiet time will help them perform better at work or be a more attentive friend.

Your Wiring Is Your Wisdom

Figure 2.3 summarizes the insights covered in this chapter. The takeaways I think are most helpful in learning how to optimize our introversion include the following:

- Introverted brains are optimized for internal thinking and analyzing.
    - Extroverted brains are optimized for external stimuli.
- Introverts think before they speak and need more quiet time after social interaction.
    - Extroverts can't help but to think and talk at the same time and crave more stimuli.
- Introverted brains are hooked on acetylcholine, connected with calm and relaxation.

   - Extroverted brains are hooked on dopamine from external stimuli, such as socializing.
- Introverted brains can be more quickly overwhelmed by external stimuli.
   - Extroverted brains are more rewarded and energized by external stimuli.

Because of these differences, we introverts can never become extroverts (and we shouldn't try!).

	Brain Differences	Challenges	Advantages
Deep Thinking	Thicker prefrontal cortex More gray and white matter Longer brain pathways	Difficult to think and act on the spot Think before we speak Takes longer to access words and ideas	Deeper thinkers in planning, analysis, introspection, connecting ideas, and accessing past experience
Observer's Edge	More blood flow to prefrontal cortex	More rumination and introspection	Strong observer and can see and interpret facial gestures, tone, what is not being said, etc., that others may not
Strategic Energy Management	More sensitive to dopamine, neurotransmitter connected to rewards Higher base level of activation in our brains	Leads to overstimulation and energy depletion in situations with people, noise, crowds Socializing requires higher cognitive load to observe, analyze, judge	More aware of energy drains so can prepare for socially draining events and reenergize
Methodical Planner	Higher concentration of glutamate (learning and memory) neurotransmitters in parts of the brain associated with planning, problem-solving, and inhibition	Risk averse	Able to see and plan for risks and able to control impulses
Powerfully Quiet	More bloodflow to acetylcholine pathways Prefer calming parasympathetic nervous system vs. action-oriented sympathetic	Prefer quiet time to heavy stimulation or socializing	Naturally find quiet time to think and create

Figure 2.3: Summary of differences, challenges, and advantages of having an introverted brain

The story behind introversion needs to change from negative to positive by emphasizing what we are great at. Focusing on our unique strengths that bring value to the world creates a powerful message. We do need to adjust our behaviors to ensure our voice is being heard. We don't need to change who we are. But we *can* change some behaviors. Use your strengths as an introvert generated by your unique brain make-up. These are all leadership strengths. And the challenges result in the perception that you are "quiet." You do not have to change your natural preference; just change behaviors like speaking up to share your leadership strengths with the world.

OUR WIRING IS OUR WISDOM, NOT OUR OBSTACLE.

Your introverted tendencies are completely normal and driven by the differences in your brain. And again, understand that introverts are not failed extroverts. Introverts: Stop spending your energy trying to be something you will never be. Be proud of your introversion. Your brain is different, and it is normal. Half the world is like you, even if you don't realize it.

I've seen in myself and my introverted clients how liberating it is to know that introverted brains are wired differently than extroverted brains. But that does not mean we can't adapt how we show up in the world. Rather, I want us all to embrace the idea that our wiring is our wisdom, not our obstacle. (See Figure 2.4.)

When I learned the brain science behind introverts and extroverts, I realized we are just playing the roles that biology gave us. We are all normal. You can't get angry about an extrovert who talks a lot more, gaining energy from being with others. That is what their biology is telling them to do. That is what is rewarding to them. And extroverts can't get angry that introverts want to stay home and be quiet or feel uncomfortable speaking up in a meeting. That is simply *their* brain biology.

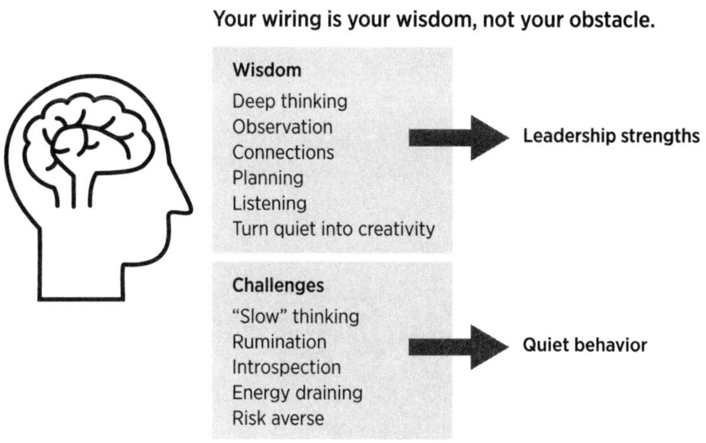

Figure 2.4: The biology of an introverted brain brings both wisdom we can build on and challenges we may need to mitigate.

Finally, keep in mind that you can build on your strengths as an introvert—deep thinking, observation, self-awareness of the need to reenergize and savor quiet time—while also modifying behaviors to be successful in a world with more extroverted ideals.

ACTIONS TO CONSIDER

If you feel inspired to take action based on this chapter, here are some ideas to get you started:

- What biological finding is most interesting to you and why?
- What one tendency of an introvert brain do you think helps you the most on the job or in your personal life? What challenges do you face because of it?
- What one introvert behavior do you think is holding you back on the job or in your personal life? What is the biological explanation for this behavior? What would it mean to you if you could change the behavior while staying true to your introverted brain?

continued

- If you were challenged to behave more like an extrovert, how would you respond?

If it helps, download the *Lead with Quiet Confidence Workbook* at www.JenniferMarcou.com/resources to help you to capture your thoughts on these and other reflection questions.

3

Leading the Changes You Want to Make

Every small positive change we make in
ourselves repays us in confidence in the future.
—Alice Walker

In my first job out of business school, I got feedback that I was the "Ice Queen" because I never smiled or said hello to coworkers in the hall. I thought that was strange, because I am the furthest thing from an Ice Queen, as I consider myself friendly and casual (at least among people I know). But, still, I heard the feedback. My behavior was giving off the Ice Queen impression, and that perception was hurting my ability to connect with others and collaborate, according to my boss. This was something I wanted to change and required me to adjust.

Being the analytical person I am, I decided to experiment and created a goal of saying hello to five people every morning. The number did not matter, but the choice in changing the behavior did. It was a small enough goal that was easy to do. It was measurable, so I knew when I'd done it and when I hadn't. At first, it was annoying because it was another to-do item. But over time, I began to enjoy saying hello to coworkers. People's reactions to me were much friendlier. Suddenly, it was no longer a to-do item but part of my natural behavior.

In the last chapter, we learned that the introverted brain is different from the extroverted brain, explaining our preferences for being quiet, which can sometimes detrimentally impact our careers. What I realized from this experience was that I didn't have to change who I was but rather could *change my behavior* to get a result I wanted. (Plus, I started building a friendlier reputation at work.) The message to all us introverts is that we don't have to become an extrovert to succeed. Rather, by changing a few behaviors, we enable ourselves to have more impact using our strengths while staying authentically true to ourselves.

In this chapter, I will share a learning framework that helps introverts make progress toward changing behaviors that are holding them back, and get you started on a voyage of change by helping you identify small steps to get you started, just as I did by saying hello to five people.

Moving from Comfort to Discomfort (and Back Again)

Neuroscience teaches us that our brains have plasticity, the ability to change. New neurons can be grown up until death. New connections can be made. But as we learned in the last chapter, we introverts will likely equate "change" with "risk." So the trick for us is finding a way to reduce the risk as we navigate the changes we want.

Growth is about getting more comfortable with the things that make you uncomfortable in a manageable and reasonable way. Again, this does not mean you are becoming an extrovert but rather simply practicing behaviors without changing the core of who you are. According to *The Powerful Purpose of Introverts* author Holley Gerth,

"Our temperament—introversion—does not change. But our behaviors can change as we learn, grow and adapt." Your general personality will not change, but you can learn new behaviors and perspectives if you put your mind to it.

A model I've found useful for thinking about this approach to change is shown in Figure 3.1, which shows a series of concentric circles that represent different zones of comfort. The innermost circle, Zone 1, represents behaviors that you are most comfortable doing. Zone 2 are behaviors that might create a little discomfort as you do them. The outermost circle, Zone 3, are behaviors that you would feel most uncomfortable about and that might increase anxiety. They are not behaviors that come naturally to you (at least not yet).

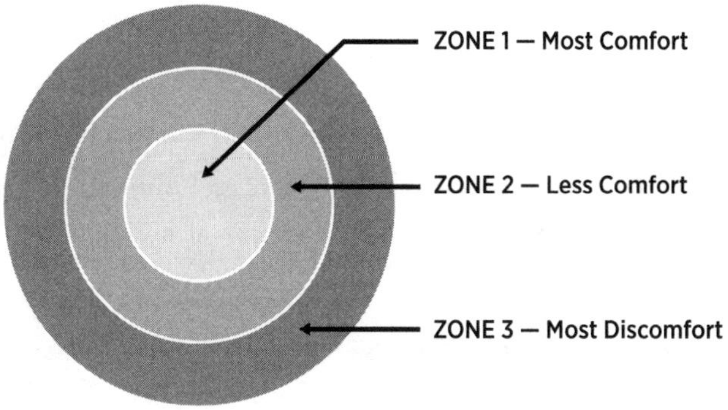

Figure 3.1: Comfort and discomfort zones

To use this model, start by identifying a goal you want to achieve, then identify small steps that will take you from Zone 1 to Zone 3 in a way that allows you to create comfort in situations that you originally find uncomfortable. For example, suppose you want to speak up in meetings. Originally, you find it is easy to speak up with your boss one-on-one but feel mild discomfort when speaking in front of a small group of people you know. And you have the most discomfort when speaking in front of a larger audience of people you don't know or who are more senior to you or you perceive to know more than you. Your diagram of this situation would look like Figure 3.2.

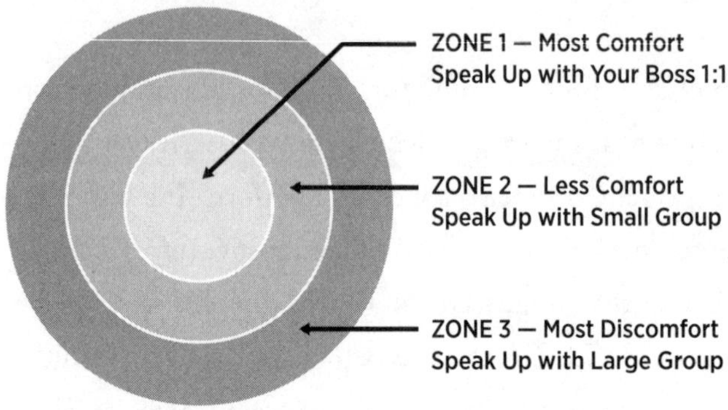

Figure 3.2: Comfort/discomfort with speaking up

The key to successful change is to think about small steps you can take that will eventually move you from Zone 1 to Zone 3 and allow you to become more comfortable at each stage along the way. Table 3.1 shows some example actions introverts I've known (including myself) describe as slightly uncomfortable (Zone 2) or very uncomfortable (Zone 3).

Goal	Example Zone 2 Action	Example Zone 3 Action
Present effectively and calmly	Speak to a small group	Speak to a large group
Honest exchange of ideas with higher-ups	Disagree openly with boss	Disagree openly with boss's boss
Connect with more peers and colleagues	Meet new people in a small group	Network in a large group
Speak up	Voice opinion to boss or a colleague one-on-one	Express a contrary opinion in a meeting with executives
Improved phone skills	Call an acquaintance on the phone to ask for advice	Call a stranger on the phone to ask for advice

Table 3.1: Examples of slightly uncomfortable and very uncomfortable actions by goal

Think Small, Kind Goals

If you are anything like me, you want to change lots of things: lose weight, build a successful business, be a better friend, be a better wife and mother, learn Spanish, eat healthy. When I try to do these all at once, I either fail or I give up. I don't want you to do that. I want you to be successful in making the changes you want to make.

That's why when thinking about changing behavior, you have to have the mindset of how to develop comfort with things that currently make you uncomfortable. The best way to make that happen is to start by identifying the smallest thing you can do to change your behavior.

So let me introduce the concept of Kind goals. These are goals that are so easy, it will be a no-brainer to complete them. The concept is not new:

- In *Atomic Habits*, James Clear calls this approach "make it easy."
- Sabina Nawaz, executive coach and *You're the Boss* author, calls them "micro habits."
- B. J. Fogg, a social scientist and author, calls them "tiny habits."

I use the label "Kind goal" to convey the idea that we need to be kind to ourselves when approaching changes that an introvert may find uncomfortable. However you describe it, brain science tells us if we make an action small enough, we are more likely to do it. In Figure 3.3, I used my own experiences to illustrate the difference between a Kind goal and "not Kind" goal. When I decided to shed the label of Ice Queen, I could have decided to try many things all at the same time, like speaking up in all meetings and saying hello to everyone, but that would have set me up for failure. If one time I did not achieve all of those goals, I would have given up. Bye-bye goal and bye-bye change I wanted to make. So instead, I set a Kind goal of saying hello to five people every day. Simple. Easy. No-brainer.

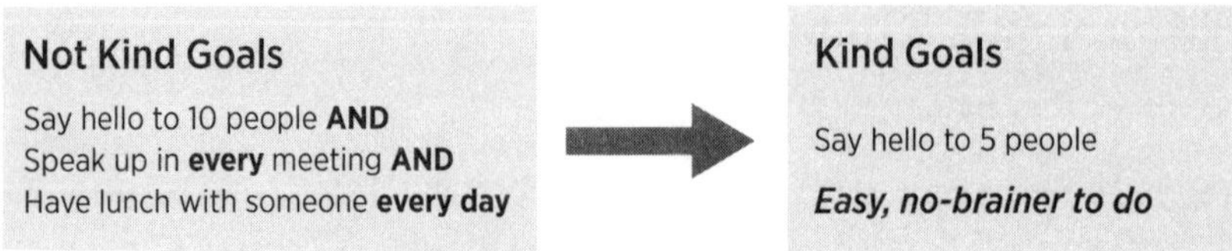

Figure 3.3: Kind and not Kind goals

More importantly, having that Kind goal set me up for success. I got comfortable with saying hello to five people, which was an accomplishment that I celebrated. In celebrating even small successes, we are more likely to do them again. Eventually, I expanded my comfort zone to the point that actions originally in my Zone 2 and even Zone 3 became second nature.

You might think that setting Kind goals is being too easy on yourself. That is good. It should be easy. You might feel like you will not make any progress with such easy goals. But you *will* make progress. You are helping your brain get used to the feeling of speaking up once a week. As that gets easier, you can increase it to twice a week, three times a week, etc. Don't push yourself too hard too fast. The key is to make it kind—a no-brainer, a layup—because that will make you most likely to continue to do that behavior. You are not going to change if you give up.

KIND GOALS CREATE SIGNIFICANT OUTCOMES.

As you keep moving forward, you can connect newly developed small habits into bigger routines. It is akin to the minimal viable product concept in engineering, where you create a prototype that moves you toward the goal you want to achieve but is not the robust end product. What is also key here is that you have to learn from each step to inform your next step. And that's how Kind goals create significant outcomes.

Why Experimenting with Behavior Is Important

The approach of stringing together a lot of small changes to create big changes is based in a psychological concept called exposure therapy. When you fear a situation, if you expose yourself to that experience in small doses and continue to increase the exposure, the fear will be reduced. You are breaking the pattern of fear associated with that behavior. For example, researchers at the University of Sussex and the University of Pennsylvania found "it takes just a week of regularly approaching new people to start getting over our fears of talking to strangers and to recognize that most interactions are far less awkward and more rewarding than we think."

To get started, you first have to identify and think about the behavior you want to change and what behavior you would prefer to take. Psychologist William James said, "Thinking is for doing." In other words, when you think of doing something, it activates the same brain region that you are using when you *actually* do something. PET brain scans confirm this. Thinking about doing something and actually doing something are neurologically similar. So use your brain to think about what you want to do, and that will prime it for when you do take the action.

As you think about the changes you want to make, use the science of behavior change. Imagine the behaviors you want to exhibit and expose yourself to experiments in areas you want to work on. And always start with creating Kind goals.

When you experiment with new behaviors, you can inspire others. Richard Restak, doctor and author, expands on the idea of mirror neurons in his book *The Naked Brain*. The brain mirrors other people's behaviors, like smiling at a baby to make them smile. Restak takes this idea further, using science to back up his claim that watching someone else take action activates your same neurons as if you took the action. By observing extroverts and their behaviors, your brain is lit up in the same way. It makes it easier to select the behaviors you want to try and experiment with them, as your brain has already been activated. Furthermore, by taking action, you are altering someone else's brain through their observations of you. By experimenting with new ways to behave (such as speaking up), you are inspiring other introverts to experiment with speaking up as well.

What Can Help You Experiment?

I use a variety of tools in my coaching to help people experiment with behavior change. The tools all work, but to different degrees for different people. But it is hard to identify which tools will be right for you without first having a conversation. So I want to expose you to a couple of frameworks that have been helpful to my clients. Here are four that I've found helpful for introverts:

- Mel Robbins has the "Let Them Theory" (and the accompanying "Let Me Theory"). She recommends recognizing what is bothering you and "letting" the other person have their thoughts and feelings while also giving yourself permission to react any way you want. So you say to yourself, *Let them [do this or feel that]* and then *Let me [feel this or do that]*. It is about how we can stop giving power to other people to control how we feel ("let them" have their feelings and we'll stop worrying about what others think or do). That allows us to regain control of ourselves ("let me" focus on what matters to me).
- Shirzad Chamine advocates for what he calls "positive intelligence." He asks us to become aware of our saboteurs, negative thoughts, and behaviors, and through mindful breathing and being in the present moment, move to embrace the Sage—the

wise, cool, calm, collected way of thinking and acting that exists within all of us.

- Tara Mohr, in her *Playing Big* book, teaches you to identify your Inner Critic, the negative voice in your head, and counteract it with various strategies, including identifying your Inner Mentor, your wiser self in twenty years.
- Jill Bolte Taylor, in her book *Whole Brain Living*, talks about the four characters of the brain and moving from the negative, fearful part of your brain to any of the other three parts, including the rational, the playful/creative, and the intuitive/spiritual ones.

In every one of these frameworks, there is an awareness of something that you want to change, something that is bothering you, and then a choice to make that change in behavior, mindset, emotion, and/or action. This is not changing who you are but rather changing your perspective, which can lead to the action you want to take. In later chapters, we will cover specific areas like speaking up, becoming more visible, having executive presence, networking, and more. All of these areas may require you to get out of your comfort zone and essentially "say it, send it, show up."

CHOOSING TO CHANGE YOUR BRAIN

What all of the tools I teach have in common is the underlying assumption that you can choose how your brain works. You can choose your behaviors, and you can choose your mindset. But you don't have to change who you are. In order to choose, you need to become aware of that behavior or feeling that you want to change, and then you have to choose to change. That choice will drive action.

Introducing the LEAD with Quiet Confidence Framework for Change

In this book, I use my own LEAD with Quiet Confidence Framework to provide a blueprint to make the changes you want to make. LEAD is an acronym that stands for

- **Learn.** These are the areas or goals you want to work on, like speaking up or getting better at networking.
- **Experiment** in behavior you want to change. Again, make these experiments Kind—something you are sure you will do.
- **Assess** the results and impact of your experiment and celebrate. How did it go? What did you learn? Celebrating is an important part of the process, but it does not need to be loud or with other people. You can celebrate in your own introverted way, such as patting yourself on the back or giving yourself a reward of a walk outside, a piece of chocolate, or putting aside fifteen minutes in the day to read.
- **Develop.** Create a plan to integrate learnings into your development. Take your learnings and repeat the behavior if it worked well. Or change the behavior if you want to improve on it. Or retry the behavior if you think it could work but did not the first time. Or stop the behavior.

An easy-to-remember version of the model is shown in Figure 3.4.

Learn – What is your goal you want to work on?

Experiment – What is something kind/easy you want to try?

Assess – How did it go? How did you celebrate taking the action?

Develop – What do you want to integrate into your life?

Figure 3.4: The LEAD with Quiet Confidence Framework

The LEAD with Quiet Confidence Framework is a repeatable process to continue to learn and evolve your habits and perspective while staying true to your authentic self. Experiment with your tactics, not your truth. When the behavior is integrated into your day-to-day, repeat all these steps with a new goal. Don't rush too quickly into the new behavior. It can take time to change a behavior.

As I mentioned in the beginning of this chapter, earlier in my career when I was called an Ice Queen, I set my mind to a learning goal (to change people's impression of me). I identified a Kind goal or experiment that was easy to do to address this (saying hello five times every morning). I assessed the impact (people seemed friendlier to me, and I realized it was not that hard and it felt good). I don't think I consciously celebrated, but I know I felt good when I accomplished it most days. Then I integrated it into my daily life, as it helped change my colleagues' impressions of me from an Ice Queen to the friendly, approachable person that I am.

Here are three reasons the LEAD with Quiet Confidence Framework works:

1. **You are taking action**, no matter how small. Neuroscience tells us that any movement forward is progress and is motivating, enabling you to repeat the action.
2. **You are assessing and modifying** along the way. If something does not work, you modify it, stop it, or do something new. Keep assessing and modifying until the behavior achieves your goal and gets more natural over time.
3. **You are celebrating taking the action.** Neuroscience tells us that celebration rewards the brain to repeat the behavior. That's why the point is not about celebrating only the successes but rather celebrating the fact that you took action, regardless of the

outcome. According to Melanie McNally, PsyD, in *Psychology Today*, celebrating wins is essential for maintaining motivation and improving overall life satisfaction. She wrote, "Research shows that recognizing small successes activates the brain's reward system, which releases dopamine and reinforces positive behavior. This process fosters a sense of accomplishment and progress and boosts self-efficacy and self-esteem."

The LEAD with Quiet Confidence Framework in Action: Sandra and a Planned Moment of Pause

One of my clients, Sandra, felt frazzled and overwhelmed as an HR professional, particularly during times of reorganizations and layoffs at her retail company. She wanted more time to think calmly instead of the constant barrage of information and decisions that needed to be made immediately. We worked on giving her time to pause in her day. Her LEAD with Quiet Confidence Framework looked like this:

- **Learn**: Start the morning calmly so she could think and focus on her priorities.
- **Experiment**: Her experiment was taking three minutes to take some deep breaths every morning before she looked at her to-do list or email. She originally wanted to do it every morning, but I knew this was a change in behavior and was not likely easy to do or remember. And unexpected things can happen that change our plans. So she developed the Kind goal of doing it three times a week. If she missed Monday, she had four more days to accomplish it. She also put it on her calendar to remind her.
- **Assess**: After the first week, she assessed how she did.
    - One: She did do it three times. She celebrated by making a special mango smoothie the next Monday.

    - Two: She realized how much more relaxed and focused she was by taking that time to breathe instead of jumping right into her work. She wanted to continue.

- **Develop**: After her success, she wanted to bump her goal to five times a week. I advised her to keep the goal Kind and make it so easy that it was a no-brainer. And she did. Some weeks she did it five times, and others she did it three. The Kind goal of three times removed the guilt and shame of not completing it all five times. It made her feel positive about her progress. It enabled her to give herself grace. And over time, this became her daily habit and she did not need the calendar prompting or goals. We went on to work on other areas of giving her space.

Throughout this book, I'll be providing prompts to help you identify areas where you can apply the LEAD with Quiet Confidence Framework to help expand your comfort zone, culminating in Chapter 14, which provides tips on defining your own path to action.

The Courage to Experiment

You have to have courage to make the changes you want to make. You also have to give yourself grace and empathy. Don't try to do it all at once. And if things don't work out every time, you are still doing it right. You are stretching yourself out of your comfort zone. Focus on being kind to yourself as you grow and develop.

EXPERIMENT WITH YOUR TACTICS, NOT YOUR TRUTH.

Experiment with your tactics, not your truth. You don't have to change who you are but just experiment with your behaviors.

ACTIONS TO CONSIDER

If the quick exercise with comfort zones and Kind goals has whetted your appetite for action, here are some other steps to consider:

- Review the tools from this chapter (the comfort/discomfort zones model, LEAD model, Kind goals). Which do you think will help you the most as you contemplate change?
- Review the goals you identified in the chapter. Confirm that these are your priorities. You can refer to these throughout the book to help you choose what behaviors you want to change and why.
- What part of the LEAD with Quiet Confidence Framework do you think you'll find most challenging? (Learn, experiment, assess, develop.) What could you do to make it easier to perform that task?
- Set another Kind (easy-to-do) goal and use the LEAD with Quiet Confidence Framework to experiment with a behavior change.
- Capture your thoughts by downloading the *Lead with Quiet Confidence Workbook* at www.JenniferMarcou.com/resources.

Part I Tool Review

Tools to Help Increase Awareness

- Review the definition of *introversion*, the workplace *consequences of being introverted*, and the *attributes* that are useful for leadership.
- Identify your strengths as an introvert.
- Identify negative definitions you've accepted about introversion, understand the biological basis for them, and reframe them to focus on the strength and contribution.
- Identify a quiet leader and their attributes you admire and incorporate those into your own repertoire.
- Identify your comfort/discomfort zones.
- Frame next steps in terms of Kind goals.
- Review the LEAD with Quiet Confidence Framework for making changes (learn, experiment, assess, develop).

PART II

CONFIDENCE: How to Build and Exude Confidence

Scott Barry Kaufman, an esteemed psychologist, author, and educator renowned for his contributions to the field of human potential and self-actualization, states this about confidence: "The most important attitude we have may be the attitude we have toward ourselves. A basic sense of self-worth and confidence in the effectiveness of our actions provides a fundamental foundation for growth."

Confidence is a critical building block to being successful as an introverted leader. Over half of my clients are looking specifically to build confidence. (They also mention communication, influencing, and visibility, all of which are connected to confidence.)

This situation isn't surprising since many introverts receive feedback at work that they don't project confidence. The challenge here is twofold: First, there is the matter of perception. Introverts may not *be* less confident than extroverts, but our natural behaviors may be *perceived* as less confident. For example, when we take more time to answer a question (because we are being thoughtful and reflective), we may appear less confident. Second, there are times when we don't feel confident even if we've put in the effort to understand an idea and articulate our thoughts.

In the following chapters, I hope to convince you that confidence can be learned, and I will explain the science behind what it takes to be perceived as a confident introvert. These chapters are relevant to all humans, but they are an important building block to making the changes you want to make as an introvert to be more successful. You should walk away with a clearer path to finding your own inner confidence to be who you are the best way you can be.

4

Competence, Meet Confidence

When you undervalue what you do,
the world will undervalue who you are.
—Oprah Winfrey

You've likely been there before. In a meeting, someone presents an idea confidently, but it might not be as innovative or effective as your idea, which you may have presented less confidently. People are likely to follow the idea that was confidently stated instead of the more competent idea. How frustrating! How many times has that happened to you? I know it has happened to me, and I have seen others go through this.

We as introverts may find this confusing because we focus more on competence, spending time researching and perfecting our ideas. We may feel the substance of a comment is more important than the delivery.

Yet we all know people who are very confident, who get the attention. Other people jump behind their ideas, even if they are not the smartest or the best ones.

What we introverts have to realize is that, as research tells us, confidence is more important than competence when it comes to attributes valued in leadership (Figure 4.1). Katty Kay and Claire Shipman, authors of *The Confidence Code*, state, "Success correlates more closely with confidence than it does with competence."

Figure 4.1: Confidence outweighs competence in perception of leadership.

Whether we are competent or not, our quietness can be interpreted as a lack of confidence. No wonder our ideas are not listened to and we feel frustrated—because confidence wins. Confidence opens doors to opportunities. People gravitate to others who are more confident. Confidence can be perceived as competence. Confidence also brings a willingness to take a chance. All of these things make people more likely to be influenced by people who are confident than those who are not.

CONFIDENCE IS MORE IMPORTANT THAN COMPETENCE.

This does not mean competence is unimportant. It means that confidence is a critical complement to it. Let's talk more about what confidence is, how we gain it (if we're lacking it), and how we project it once we have it.

What Is Confidence?

Confidence is the belief that we possess the skills, abilities, and qualities necessary to achieve our desired outcomes. It is the sense of self-assurance that comes from appreciating and acknowledging our own capabilities. Confidence allows us to trust in our potential and rely on ourselves to overcome challenges and succeed. Confidence can enhance your success, while a lack of confidence can undermine it.

Confidence Is Built Through Action

Confidence is tied to action. People who feel confident are more likely to get out of their comfort zone. Confidence enables us to take a risk and not play it safe all the time. On the flip side, confidence is built by taking action.

The Confidence Code authors Kay and Shipman state, "Failure is a critical partner of confidence and the inevitable result of risk-taking and it's essential for building resilience." Each time you fail, you are building resilience, creating opportunity for new innovation, and developing new pathways for your growth. So we must push ourselves out of our comfort zone and allow ourselves to fail in order to build that confidence.

Confidence allows us to explore new behaviors that may not be natural for us, such as asking for a promotion or raising a differing opinion. Confidence turns your thoughts into actions. By thinking of taking action and actually taking action, you are building your confidence. For example, by thinking of the value you provide in your job and sharing that with your boss to ask for a promotion, you are taking a thought and turning it into an action of asking to be paid your value. And the action increases your confidence versus wallowing in thinking you should be promoted.

Scott Barry Kaufman, author of *Transcend*, connects the dots between action and confidence: "The more successful you are at making progress toward your goals, the more confident you feel, and the two tend to spiral upward toward a stable sense of mastery." (See Figure 4.2.)

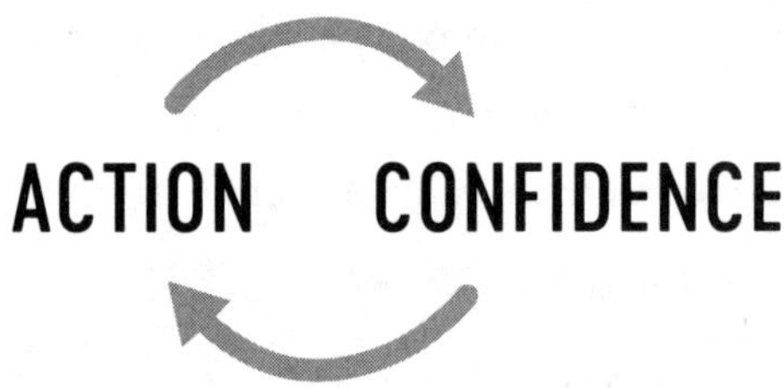

Figure 4.2: Action builds confidence and vice versa.

That said, confidence does not always have to look the same. You can show quiet confidence; it does not need to be loud and boisterous.

But to succeed in building confidence, we introverts have to be working on something that is important to us. Caroline Miller, author and coach, states, "Confidence comes from stepping out of your comfort zone and working toward goals that come from your own values and needs; goals that aren't determined by society." For example, your own personal development goals that are important to you are going to be much more impactful in building your confidence than achieving a milestone promotion that your boss defines. These two goals can be one and the same. But if the goal is driven from within (versus external goals that others define for you), you will grow your confidence even further as it becomes personal.

Special Confidence Challenges for Women

If you are a woman, whether introverted or extroverted, confidence sometimes seems more elusive when compared to men. According to research by Joyce Ehrlinger and David Dunning of Cornell University, "Women performed equally to men on a science quiz, yet underestimated their performance because they thought less of their general scientific reasoning ability than did men. They, consequently, more likely refused to enter a science competition." Women were found in this research study to hold themselves back due to their lower confidence in their abilities even when they had the same abilities as men.

In addition, according to another research study from Columbia Professor Ernesto Reuben, in 2011, "Men consistently rated their past performance about 30% higher than it really was. Women, on the other hand, consistently rated their past performance only about 15% higher than it actually was." Women are not inflating their past performance as much as men are. You can imagine the impact in job interviews when a woman is up against a man.

Introverted women have an even greater challenge. As female introverts who are not strong at self-promotion (or prefer not to do it at all), we have to push doubly hard to feel confident internally and show confidence externally.

CONFIDENCE IS TEACHABLE, NOT UNREACHABLE.

How Much Can We Change Our Confidence?

Some people believe that confidence is innate: You either have it or you don't. In fact, research shows that only 50 percent of confidence comes from our genes; the other 50 percent can be learned (see Figure 4.3). It is a choice—remember, the brain has plasticity, which means it can change as we learn new behaviors. Confidence is teachable, not unreachable.

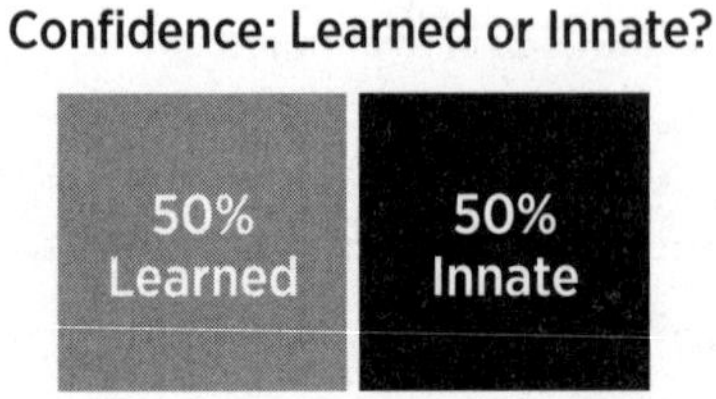

Figure 4.3: Confidence is teachable.

I am sure you can imagine situations in your past where you were not confident, and now, after having learned a new skill or experienced the situation more frequently, you are much more confident. For me, I am much more confident than I used to be in chitchatting with people in line in the grocery store or meeting a new person at a party. We tend to focus on things we are not confident in. But reflect on the things you are now confident in and appreciate your growth.

How do we grow our confidence internally as well as people's perception of our confidence externally?

The Basics of Building and Projecting Confidence

Later chapters will provide specific tactics you can use to cultivate and project confidence in specific situations, but here are six principles you can use in any situation:

1. Calm your fears through exposure.
2. Find an alternative way to achieve a goal.
3. Learn skills that will help you.
4. Prepare and practice.
5. Rewrite the negative stories in your brain.
6. Have conviction.

1. Calm Your Fears Through Exposure

When I was five, I used to fly by myself to visit my grandparents. I thought this was completely normal. It wasn't until I became older that I realized how unique I was in having that type of independence at that young age. I now realize it gave me a lot of confidence, especially when traveling. And it informed things I did with my own children to foster their confidence and independence being in the world.

Growing my confidence and independence was important to my parents. When I was in middle school, my parents made me order the pizza when we had takeout. It was a small task, and I was completely capable of doing it, but boy, I hated having to talk to strangers on the phone, even when the dialogue was very well defined, like ordering pizza. To this day, I still hate ordering food on the phone. I usually ask my husband to call for takeout and handle calls to customer service. But again, that early forced exposure to calling strangers showed me that I *can* do things that are uncomfortable. It gave me confidence that I could speak to strangers even though it was not my favorite thing to do.

The exposure theory approach is one way to achieve the goal I talked about in a previous chapter of moving out of your comfort zone. It is a way to reduce your fear of something new or different and at the same time build confidence. Perhaps an action you could take may not be the most pleasant thing, like speaking to a customer service agent live versus trying to resolve an issue online. But for me, I just kept exposing myself to my discomfort zone, like presenting, and it became easier because my fears reduced and my confidence increased.

2. Find an Alternative Way to Achieve a Goal

I went through a training program where I had to identify five things I could be doing in my career in five years. One of my ideas was to have a coaching and leadership business but without the business development parts.

At the time, I thought there was no way I could create a successful new business without doing sales. The idea of cold-calling strangers was definitely in my "most uncomfortable" zone.

My solution was to find a way to achieve the end goal of generating sales that stayed true to my introvert nature and avoided traditional sales activities. What do I like to do as an introvert? Have deep conversations one-on-one.

So when I actually started my coaching business four years later, I reached out to contacts on LinkedIn who I would be interested in coaching and asked to catch up. It helped that it was the start of COVID, in 2020, and people were confused, working from home, and assessing their lives.

During these conversations, I would never say the dreaded salesy words, "Do you or someone you know need a coach?" Instead, I would ask curious questions about their lives. I would have a deep conversation on how they were surviving COVID and how they were feeling about their career. Inevitably, they would ask what I was doing. And usually in the last three minutes of the call they would say they needed a coach. And voilà, I had a client prospect.

The exposure principle came into play here as well. I was extremely uncomfortable during the first calls I made, especially when people asked me what I charged. But with more and more calls under my belt, I looked at it as a conversation with a colleague, not a sales call. I grew to enjoy the calls—even the parts about how much I charge. (Hint—tell the investment cost and then stop talking.) The more exposure I had, the easier it became.

3. Learn Skills That Will Help You

When I was in business school, I hated doing presentations, but they were a core part of the curriculum. Knowing the concepts was just as important as convincing others of your ideas. We would have group projects in almost every class and had to present on a marketing idea or company stock evaluation to the rest of the class for ten to twenty minutes to thirty to fifty people. We were graded on both written content as well as content and style of presentation, preparing us for the world of business where we would have to influence others no matter what area of business we chose.

I knew mastering presentations like those was critical to success in school as well as in the workplace. So I decided I needed to learn more about the skills needed to make effective presentations, and I joined Toastmasters. It is a wonderful program where you create a presentation and practice it in front of an audience. You are also videotaped. I created presentations about a learning experience at work and a time I had to overcome a challenge.

At first, it was dreadful to watch myself present and listen to the sound of my voice. But the more I did it, the more comfortable I got in this discomfort zone (exposure therapy surfaces again!). And I learned some real skills and strategies to be a more effective presenter, including telling stories and not bobbing my head. I got to the point where I could present well in front of my team, senior leaders, and larger groups of strangers.

Now when I watch a recording of myself, I don't cringe. I can objectively look at my presentation and recognize what I did well and what I could do differently. I have much more confidence in my presentations because I took the time to learn more skills and get used to watching myself.

4. Prepare and Practice

There is a level of discomfort that comes any time we try a new skill or do anything new. For us introverts, preparation and practice are key to decreasing the discomfort and increasing confidence. When learning to do presentations, for example, preparation and practice allowed me to improve the speed with which I responded to questions. Now, before any presentation, I identify likely questions and prepare responses.

Preparation and practice are another way to overcome the perceptions of lack of confidence introverts have in their slower (but more thoughtful) response times. Arthur Ashe, tennis champion and humanitarian, once stated, "An important key to self-confidence is preparation." So, practice, practice, practice and "it"—whether that be giving presentations or asking for a raise or asking for a special project—will become easier, and you will feel more confident.

5. Rewrite the Negative Stories in Your Brain

We often tell ourselves negative stories about who we are or what we can do. For example, most of my life I told myself, *I'm not a runner.* I failed the running test in high school when we had to run a mile in fifteen minutes. I thought that was an impossibility. I also told myself I did not have the body type to be a runner. But at some point in my adult life, I looked at that belief, that story, and said that is not true. I started to run (well, *jog*, as my husband would say). I put myself out there on the streets day after day. I did my first 5K and worked up to 10K and after about ten years, I ended up doing two half marathons. I could no longer say I was not a runner. I had rewritten that story.

The negative stories about ourselves sap confidence and keep us from taking risk (i.e., acting confidently!). In the previous story about reaching out to people on LinkedIn to start my coaching business, I rewrote the story that I hate business development. In my mind, I was not doing prospecting calls; I was connecting with past colleagues. But in the end, it was business development, just on my terms.

Observe the stories you tell yourself. Which stories are helping you? Which stories are not? What can you do to minimize the negative stories?

6. Have Conviction

I've always told myself I am not a writer. (See item #5 above!) I've always been stronger in the sciences and math. I hated writing papers in high school and college. Yet I decided to write a book, a fact my younger self would say was completely crazy. What allowed me to overcome that negative story? It was my passion to help other introverts, my conviction that I have something of value to share. Now I *am* a writer!

When you have conviction in what you want to say, you can feel more confident. If you have a strong opinion on something and feel you cannot hold back stating your thoughts, you are likely to feel confident in speaking up. Remember the story in Chapter 1 about Mahatma Gandhi speaking out about his views of the British government after a childhood where he'd run home from school so he did not have to talk to anyone? Because he felt so strongly about doing the right thing for his country and mankind, he was able to speak up. If you have the skills or strengths on a particular topic, you are more likely to be more confident. Identifying your passions and values and how they relate to the topic you need to be more confident in can help give you confidence even in situations that are uncomfortable. It was always easier for me as a leader to ask for a promotion for someone on my team than it was to ask for a promotion for myself. I have conviction and confidence to promote my direct report. But I did not always feel the same way about myself. Having conviction can also help you overcome the external perceptions of your quietness or the time it takes to respond. With conviction, your tone of voice can get deeper and your volume louder and you can be perceived as more confident.

Letting Go of Fear: How Donna Increased Her Confidence

Donna leads a large marketing team at a big tech firm and was asked to present to the chief marketing officer. Normally this means lots of preparation of slides and many reviews with her leaders before presenting. She was getting mixed feedback about the best way to handle the presentation: Her boss wanted more details, while a colleague with experience presenting to the senior leader recommended being higher level and bringing in a more strategic perspective. Stress was causing her to lose sleep, as it felt like the stakes were high; budget and head count decisions were being made, and she wanted to put her and her team's best foot forward.

When she and I talked through her situation in a coaching session, she realized she had conviction in her perspective. She was the expert in her area. She also reminded herself that she had successfully presented to other senior leaders before. Her confusion was the multiple perspectives in how to approach the presentation and trying to please all of them. Her epiphany started with a "let them" moment; she was going to trust herself and let her boss and colleagues believe whatever they wanted.

After the coaching session, she felt empowered and calm and knew to trust her own judgment. She decided to take a risk and approach the presentation with a more Socratic method, doing more asking than telling so that the leaders could come to their own conclusions. She did her preparation, using her strength in analytical thinking, and stopped letting her anxious emotions cloud that thinking. She rewrote the story in her head that she was an appendage and mouthpiece of her boss, following exactly in his footsteps, and instead described herself as an expert and a leader. Suddenly, she was very calm and got some sleep before the presentation the next Monday.

Right before the meeting, she did a few breathing exercises to reconnect to that calm presence she'd had after our coaching session. In the presentation, she was so calm, in fact, that her Apple watch heart rate monitor thought she was sleeping. She let her conviction in her perspective shine through. While she cared about what her bosses thought, she did not let that impact her performance.

The meeting was a success. Despite not following all the recommendations her boss made for the presentation, he said she did a great job and trusted her leadership. This was a huge win for the business and, more importantly, for Donna. She trusted herself to know how to approach the presentation and to let go of her fears of what other people thought. She rewrote her story of herself as a leader. She allowed herself to truly shine with her introversion and all. She did not need to be the loudest person in the room. She showed up with conviction that she had an important perspective.

How can we do what Donna did? Reflect on the questions and actions below, and continue reading the next few chapters to find your own inner confidence.

Confidence Is More than Competence

Confidence is the belief that you can be successful. Confidence is also the key to your success as an introvert, either building confidence internally or compensating for perceptions of lack of confidence due to your quiet and thoughtful nature. Confidence is all of the following:

- Belief in yourself
- A choice you make
- Tied to action
- More important than competence

The good news is that confidence can be learned. Confidence comes from actions. So, take actions; even small steps will lead to learning and resilience, which will build confidence.

If you are not confident internally, it is important as an introvert to build your confidence to be able to move out of your comfort zone to behave in ways you want to. And even if you are generally confident, there are times, such as being in new situations or being with new people, when you may not feel confident. Exposing yourself to discomfort, rewriting your stories, and practicing and having conviction may seem easy to do on paper, but they can be difficult in practice. In the next three chapters, we will work on building your internal strength to help you put these into practice.

ACTIONS TO CONSIDER

If you feel inspired to take action based on this chapter, here are some ideas to get you started.

- Think about when you feel confident and when you don't. What's the difference?
- Reflect on skills you've learned that have made you more confident. What other skills could you learn that would increase your confidence in other settings?
- Pay attention to the stories you're telling yourself in your head—especially negative ones that are draining your confidence. Rewrite one of those stories.

- What is an upcoming situation that you don't feel confident about? What could you do to prepare or practice that would help ease your fears?
- Use the LEAD with Quiet Confidence Framework to test out an action that will get you closer to the confidence you want: Identify your **l**earning objective, **e**xperiment, **a**ssess and celebrate, and **d**evelop. Continue to take that action and watch your confidence grow over time.

If it helps, download the *Lead with Quiet Confidence Workbook* at www.JenniferMarcou.com/resources to help you to capture your thoughts on these and other reflection questions.

5

Finding Confidence Through Your Inner Compass

What lies behind us and what lies before us
are tiny matters compared to what lies within us.
—Ralph Waldo Emerson

In the year before I left my corporate role to become a coach, I did an exercise in a leadership class to identify my values. I had done something similar several times before, and my values had never changed. So it was begrudgingly that I did the exercise this time. And lo and behold, two of my top five values had changed. *Achievement* and *respect* were no longer in my top five. They were replaced by *development* and *awe*.

My first reaction was to wonder whether I had been lying to myself all those years that I'd felt achievement and respect were important. But no, in fact, I had wanted to climb the corporate ladder, and values of achievement and respect had helped me do that. Now I had changed. I wanted to focus on development and awe. Development made sense, as I was always passionate about developing myself and developing others. But I had no idea what to make of *awe*. What is awe in the workplace? The more coaching I did, the more I realized how awe fits into the work environment. I feel awe when a light bulb goes off in my client's mind that they have a choice in the way they think or when they take what they think is a risky move by speaking up and nothing bad happens. I feel awe as I witness their development and journey.

As it turned out, this new interest in development and awe contributed to my decision a year later to leave corporate life and become a leadership coach. It was a big risk moving from a comfortable corporate leadership position to starting a business with no paying clients. Logically and economically, it did not make sense.

I was lucky, however, that over the years, I had picked up tools, models, and experiences that have all kept me grounded in my authentic self and helped me move to the next step of where I am supposed to and want to go. I began to see how five specific components of confidence and authenticity came together in what I call the Inner Compass. These components have helped me with big changes as I transitioned from corporate leader to coach, then added on the roles of author and speaker. My Inner Compass has helped me with everything, from the smaller decisions of how to handle a conflict in a relationship to overcoming a mistake I made (or thought I had made) to showing up confidently as my true self in places that make me uncomfortable, such as at large meetings. Exploring the components has helped me understand how our brains are much more powerful and more controllable than we realize and showed me more pathways for making self-confidence learnable.

In this chapter, I'll introduce you to the Inner Compass and explain how focusing on these elements can help guide you too.

Five Components of the Inner Compass

To gain confidence by being more certain about who we are and what we want, I've relied on the following five elements that compose the Inner Compass (see Figure 5.1):

1. **Mindfulness**—Being in the present moment and being aware of your emotions
2. **Intuition**—Finding and trusting your instincts
3. **Purpose**—Identifying your purpose, your reason to be, in life and in the moment
4. **Self-Compassion**—Cultivating compassion and empathy for yourself
5. **Wisdom Within**—Connecting with your true, wise self

Figure 5.1: Your Inner Compass

In my own journey, these elements came together when I faced the major change of going from corporate executive to coach (and more). I needed to practice mindfulness to keep myself rooted in the present moment instead of paralyzed by fears of the future. My intuition knew this was the right thing for me. I recognized my purpose as helping people grow as leaders; it became even more refined when I decided to focus on introverts in leadership. My fears of speaking up, writing a book as a professed nonwriter, and making speeches suddenly reduced because I started doing all those things to fulfill my purpose. Not that I feel superior or have grandiose ideas. I am just a normal person who is propelled forward by her purpose and, in the process, quieting negative thoughts. As a coach, suddenly my values, my purpose, my intuition, and my career were fully aligned. And yes, there were and still are days where I beat myself up for not doing something right or I am fearful of taking a big step. That is where I have found self-compassion to be a key tool, so I can stop criticizing myself and let mindfulness keep me present. These are underlying ways of being that support me in my journey to be my true self and create clarity of where I want to grow.

By combining these elements, I was able to identify the Wisdom Within to help me define and stay on the right path for me. In the rest of this chapter, we'll take a tour of the four ordinal points of the compass (mindfulness, intuition, purpose, and self-compassion); then in Chapter 6 we'll deep dive into the center of the compass and explore how the Wisdom Within can make us stronger, more confident leaders.

Mindfulness and the Skill to Pause

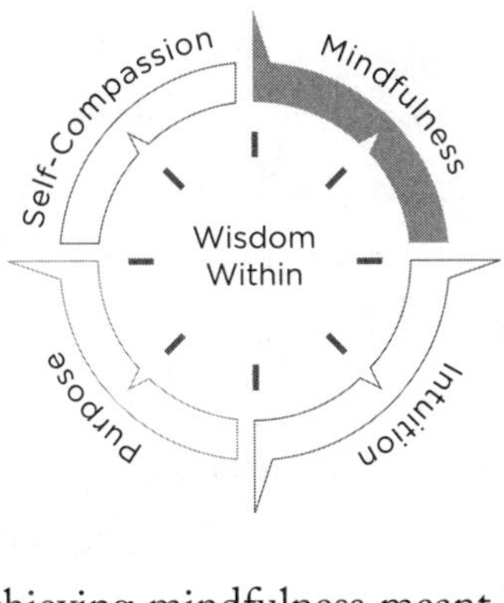

I initially thought achieving mindfulness meant having a blank mind, which I was never able to achieve (most people can't). But mindfulness is about bringing into your awareness what is happening in your mind. Mindfulness is about being aware of your thoughts and not judging them. Two ideas helped me with my own mindfulness practice:

1. It is called a mindfulness *practice*. Every time you do a mindful technique, it is a practice, not a perfection. When you are practicing mindfulness, your brain will wander. That is completely normal. The practice is bringing your mind back into awareness of the wandering and letting the thoughts go. We are always practicing—even the most experienced meditator.
2. Mindfulness is like seeing your mind as a flag on a flagpole: Sometimes that flag is gently blowing in the wind; other times, it is wagging around like in a hurricane. The point of mindfulness is to notice what your mind (or flag) is doing right now. Don't focus on the goal of making the flag stop moving. Just notice what movement or thoughts you are having and let them go. And by letting them go, I don't mean getting rid of them. They will still be there in the background. Just focus on the *noticing* of the ideas, not the ideas or thoughts themselves.

Mindfulness saved me from quitting my job. In one role in the corporate world, I had no control of a partner team whose work was critical for my team's success. The leader was aggressive and brash and created incredible stress for my team any time we interacted with him. We could not achieve any of our goals without that partner team, but instead of collaboration, it felt like it was competition. On top of that, during budget discussions, all of our project funding was in question.

The evening after a particularly challenging budget discussion, I went to see a concert with my husband, featuring Damien Rice, a soulful, moody singer. I wept during the entire concert, partly for the beautiful music and mostly because of the stress. I asked my husband, "What is the number? What amount of money do we need to save so I can leave my job?" I was so stressed out that I was ready to quit.

But then, thankfully, our corporate health center sent an email that next day about stress-management coaching. Talk about synchronicity. I signed up immediately. At the first meeting, when I described my stress, the feeling of lack of control, and challenges with a colleague, my coach said I should try "mindfulness."

I didn't really know what that was, so I proceeded to read several books on mindfulness (including the one I will recommend in the References section). I learned that mindfulness is the practice of focusing on the present moment without judgment. It is related to meditation, but it does not require you to sit for hours in a special place or position to meditate. Practicing mindfulness can be as simple as focusing on your senses, such as touching your hands and feeling all the lines in your palm or listening to a sound that is far away. Quieting the mind allows you to calm down any emotions that are triggered and recognize your creativity and that there are many different options than you think initially. Just a few minutes of mindfulness can clear your mind and enable you to access your strengths, your confidence, and different parts of the brain.

I began practicing mindfulness several times a week. My version involved closing my eyes and taking deep breaths in and out, letting any thoughts go, not judging them. It also included being very focused on my senses one at a time. I would practice twenty minutes a day four to five times a week. I found this practice would calm me immediately after, but I also found it had the longer-lasting impact of being calm throughout the day.

Gradually, this practice changed my mindset at work. I was calmer, less triggered by others—particularly the challenging colleague—more aware of what was bothering me, more courageous to have tough conversations with that colleague. I did not quit my job, and I have since been a regular practitioner of mindfulness and teach it to my clients. I am so grateful for this tough time in my life, as it helped me discover mindfulness.

In leadership, you need to make choices every day in how you react to things. Mindfulness gives you that skill to pause and make a choice instead of defaulting to old habits. Being the quiet leader you want to be requires confidence; an awareness of you, your strengths, and your goals; and being able to see the bigger picture, access your strengths, and act on your goals without the interference of your critical voices. That mindful awareness of what you are thinking and the ability to make choices helps support you being the leader you want to be.

There is lots of research on the benefits of mindfulness, from reducing anxiety and rewiring or reframing your brain to accepting the present moment (whether you like it or not). Richard Davidson, PhD, a renowned professor of psychology and psychiatry, found that a half hour a day of mindfulness for two weeks can result in brain changes.

There are also lots of wonderful books, classes, and apps out there if you want to learn how to practice mindfulness. The book that helped me start my own practice was *Mindfulness: An Eight-Week Plan for Finding Peace in a Frantic World* by Mark Williams and Danny Penman. I liked the week-by-week exercises. The key is to find a quiet moment, become aware of your breathing, and let any judgment of your thoughts go. I find that for me, becoming innately focused on my senses (sight, hearing, touch, taste, smell) enables my thoughts to quiet down. I even do this in meetings—taking three deep breaths or, in an online meeting, looking in great detail at someone's background in terms of colors, shading, and shapes.

MINDFULNESS AND INTROVERSION

As we discussed in Chapter 2, introverts have a rich internal landscape, as we spend a lot of time in our prefrontal cortex thinking. Sometimes that thinking becomes rumination, where we think too much or think only about risks or negative sides, which is unproductive. But mindfulness is one way to leverage the strength of your introverted thoughtfulness without letting it lead to rumination.

According to Arnie Kozak, author of *The Awakened Introvert*, mindfulness "can help you be more comfortable, adaptable, and flexible as an introvert." Because mindfulness promotes more neuroplasticity, that ability to change your brain to reduce negative thoughts, you can cultivate more courage and confidence to make the changes you want.

Learning to Listen to Your Intuition

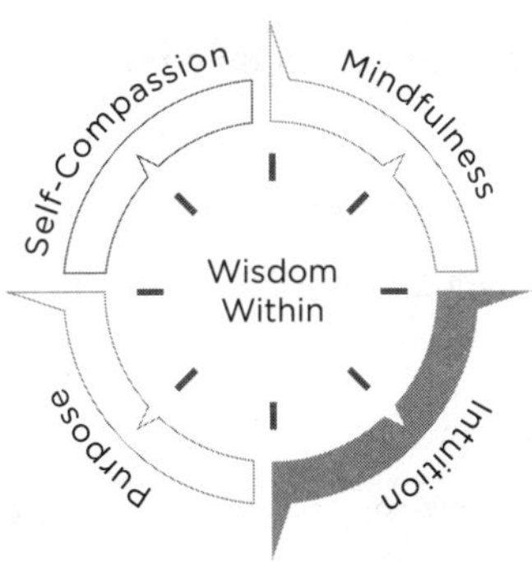

Intuition is the second component of the Inner Compass. It is the inner knowing we have even if we do not know the source of that belief. For those who can connect easily to their intuition, it comes very quickly. There is no "thinking" involved. For those who are highly rational, it may be more difficult to get in touch with or believe in that gut feeling, as it is often based on a sense, informed by past experience.

Intuition cannot be explained rationally. The rational mind knows one plus one equals two—always. The intuitive mind knows that the whole is greater than the sum of its parts. One plus one can equal more than two.

Introverts who are much more inwardly focused have the innate ability to home in on what is happening inside of them. They certainly can think through things logically with the strong deep-thinking capacity. But with practice and awareness of the multiple views inside of them, they can effectively connect to that inner knowing.

Introverts can also use their strength in listening and observation to identify what is not being said and follow their instinct to follow up with someone after a meeting. I have found myself hovering around someone after a meeting, not really sure why but just feeling like I needed to talk with them more. I'll often realize later that I was sensing some misalignment or misunderstanding. If I'd let my analytical mind lead, it would have dismissed the hunch I felt. Using our intuition and our innate introverted strengths can help build our confidence in adding value at work beyond what is said in a meeting.

Intuition is not always accurate. In fact, in unknown situations, your intuition may lean too heavily on past experiences, which may not have the full knowledge of a situation or options. But in decisions of your own development and growth, your intuition is usually right on.

You can try small experiments when your intuition recommends a certain action or decision. Test it with a low-risk action before jumping in fully. Over time, you can build your confidence in your intuition and at the same time build your confidence overall. You can also reflect on major decisions and assess whether your intuition was correct or not. Again, you will build a better understanding of where intuition can help. And remember, if data fails, trust your gut.

THE FOUR CHARACTERS OF YOUR BRAIN

Dr. Jill Bolte Taylor is a neuroanatomist who experienced a stroke in the left hemisphere of her brain. Her second book, *Whole Brain Living: The Anatomy of Choice and the Four Characters That Drive Our Life*, presents a simple model that has been especially life changing for me and my clients. Taylor says there are four main characters in your brain:

- **Character 1** is the left-thinking brain. It is the area that we typically envision when we think about the brain—analytical, rational, plans, judges, gets stuff done.
- **Character 2** is the left emotional brain. It is where the negative emotions of fear, anxiety, anger, guilt, and shame reside. Character 2 does not like new things. It represents what we fear. Its role is to keep us safe. Unfortunately, these negative emotions can take over as a critical voice that can inhibit us from doing what we really want to do. We will learn more about this in Chapter 7.
- **Character 3** is the right emotional brain. It is playful, relaxed, curious, present, empathetic, and forgiving. This part of the brain likes new things. This part of the brain is like a kid jumping into a rain puddle because it's fun. My clients talk about this brain as their vacation brain.
- **Character 4** is the right-thinking brain. It is intuitive, feels like you are connected to something bigger, spiritual, compassionate, embraces change. It accepts that everything is as it should be. It is your best self. It is your intuition, gut, sage self, or your Wisdom Within, which we will learn about in Chapter 6.

What I find most useful about this model is getting people to pause and reflect on which character of their brain they are using at any given moment and whether using a different

continued

character might be more appropriate. For example, by default, I use a lot of my Character 1 (analysis/planning). When I am on vacation, I use more of my Character 3 (curiosity). When I am coaching, I am more in my Character 4, connecting with my client and witnessing what they say and feel. When I feel self-doubt, or frankly any negative emotion, I know I am in Character 2. Unfortunately, for self-preservation, Character 2 can play an outsized role in the introverted mind, especially in rumination.

Building Confidence Through Intuitive Action: Sandy's Story

Sandy is a director at an online marketing firm. She was not feeling confident going into her year-end review with her new boss. She had had a significant impact this past year, but she had not spotlighted all of her accomplishments to her boss. Internally, she had conflicting thoughts and emotions:

- She was worried that her boss did not really know what she had worked on and feared that she would think poorly of her if Sandy plugged her accomplishments.
- She was both empathetic with her situation and wanted to avoid embarrassing her boss if she did not know all of Sandy's accomplishments.
- She wanted to have an open conversation with her boss as part of her learning and development as a leader and human and believed that if she did not speak up and did poorly on her review and received a low bonus, she would feel angry at herself for not speaking up.

Ultimately, Sandy decided to listen to her intuition and have a conversation with her boss where she shared a high-level story of her accomplishments in the past year. Her boss was very receptive and thankful for her proactivity. Sandy did get a positive and well-informed review. When I asked her what advice she would have for herself if she encountered this feeling again, she said she would want to be in the moment and listen to her gut—it had the answer.

Purpose

Research has shown that having a purpose has been connected with happiness and life satisfaction.

I think of purpose as coming in two sizes (see Figure 5.2). The "big *P*" Purpose is the answer to a large existential question, such as "Why do I exist?" As I mentioned before, one factor that gave me the confidence to make a major change in my career direction was the fact that I had defined a new Purpose (big *P*) for my work, which was helping introverts be leaders.

But defining a purpose can play a role in improving confidence and clarity every day if you think of it on a smaller scale—just like mindfulness is smaller chunks of meditation. In that way, purpose (little *p*) helps us find meaning in our everyday activities.

p	P
Little p purpose *Why am I in this meeting?* Contribute ideas Share my experience Make connections Listen and learn	**Big P Purpose** *Why am I in in this role?* *Why am I on this Earth?* Ensure the customer needs are met Contribute my gifts to the world Show kindness

Figure 5.2: Little *p* and big *P* purpose

The reason I like to think about purpose is it gives me focus and allows unimportant things—like what people think of me—to fall away. Scott Barry Kaufman, author of *Transcend*, states, "Having a purpose often causes a fundamental reordering of the most central motives associated with the self. Things that once preoccupied you suddenly cause you little concern and may even seem trivial." Focusing on your purpose allows you to let go of the distractions, let go of the critical voice in your head, and be open to your intuition and true self.

LET INTUITION HELP YOU IDENTIFY PURPOSE

As we move around the Inner Compass, the connections between its components start to become clearer. For example, intuition can play an important role to help you identify and guide you to your purpose. Just as Sandy's intuition told her that she was meant to have the conversation with her boss, as it was part of her learning in developing into a leader, you, too, can use your intuition to identify your purpose.

Defining Your Purpose (Little *p*)

Working to define a "little *p*" purpose helps you keep even the small things you're doing aligned with your Inner Compass. For example, a common complaint among all businesspeople is that they don't know why they have to attend a particular meeting. Many times, you don't know why. You can always ask the meeting organizer but may not get a satisfactory answer. When that happens to me, I define a reason for myself. Here are some common answers I come up with:

- Share my expertise on digital marketing
- Represent the interests of the customer
- Bring back new ideas for my team
- Observe how to run a meeting (or how not to run a meeting)
- Think of new ideas to solve the problem
- Collaborate with colleagues to ensure we work more effectively together

What are the reasons you normally attend meetings? If, after brainstorming your own list, you can't discover a purpose, then likely you're not really needed at the meeting. Tell the organizer why you won't be coming, and don't go unless they can come up with a convincing reason why you *should* attend. (Yeah! Reducing meetings!)

Defining a Broader Purpose (Big *P*)

There are lots of great books to help you define your broader purpose in life. Here are two books that helped me discover that coaching was what I was meant to do:

- *The Power of Story* by Jim Loehr helps you define your mission and then integrate actions to move toward your mission in your life.

- *Playing Big* by Tara Mohr helps you identify your calling—what it is that you are meant to do if you let all the titles, company, and industry drop away. What is at the heart of what you want to do and are being called to do?

There are also exercises that help you define purpose. Here's one example.

USING THE FIVE WHYS TO FIND PURPOSE

One easy method to help you dig deeper to find a purpose (little *p* or big *P*) is called the Five Whys. Start with a question such as "What is my purpose?" State your first gut-level answer, then ask the question "Why?" each time you come up with an answer. Here is an example:

- **What is your purpose?**
  I want to coach introverted leaders.
- **Why?**
  Because I feel I can help them with my experience and coaching skills.
- **Why?**
  Because I wish I'd had the knowledge I have now when I was starting in my career.
- **Why?**
  Because I would have progressed much faster and more confidently.
- **Why?**
  Because I would have been confident in my own skin and been a role model for others to do the same much sooner.

- **Why?**
  Because earlier in my life I would have been living and breathing what I teach and coach now.

As you can see, this questioning may not get you to the exact calling, but it will help you delve deeper into your answers. As you can see by my answers, I have a purpose around helping other introverts learn to be successful leaders in their own way much sooner than I did.

Self-Compassion

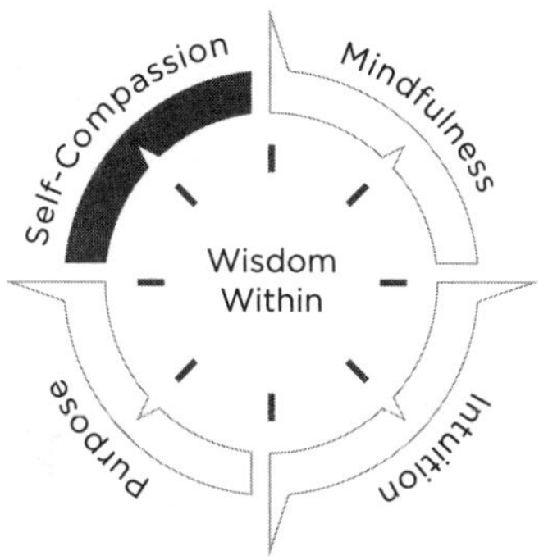

The easiest description of self-compassion is treating yourself the way you would treat a good friend, approaching yourself with understanding, empathy, and kindness. It is showing yourself support and encouragement. Because we would never say the negative things we say to ourselves to a friend, one trick is to pretend your friend is in your situation and state something empathetic to "your friend," redirecting it to yourself.

For example, if a friend told you they procrastinated on a project and they had to work on it all weekend to complete it before the deadline, you wouldn't say, "Get on it! You're so lazy!" No! (Or at least, not if you wanted to keep that friend!) You would probably say something like, "That's really hard. I procrastinate too. We all do. You are going to get through this. You've got this. And maybe next weekend when it is done, we can hang out together." That response is empathetic, supportive, and encouraging.

Empathy is the ability to understand and share the feelings of another. It can be very difficult to give yourself empathy. However, there is a formula (see Figure 5.3).

1. **Recognize the emotions you are feeling.**

   Be mindful of your thoughts and feelings around a quality or action you feel bad about, such as procrastination. Feel the guilt or shame. Feel the negative judgments you have about yourself—despite your best efforts to hide those emotions. Naming the emotion helps reduce the feeling of it in the brain.

2. **Recognize the common humanity.**

   When speaking with a friend, you would probably say something like, "No one is perfect. I have felt that too. This is completely normal." This will probably be foreign, as we are so good at saying the negative, critical things to ourselves. But what is one statement you could make to assure yourself that this is normal? I like to say to myself, "I'm only human."

3. **Encourage versus self-criticize.**

   Recognize that most negative things that we say to ourselves—like "I am not good enough" or "Nothing will ever change"—are not helpful. It only makes us feel worse. Here are alternatives:

   - Tell yourself, "It's going to be OK."
   - Remind yourself of your goal, the bigger picture, or your "why" (why you are doing this task in the broader sense). For example, when I procrastinated writing my book, I was

worried it was not going to be good enough. But my "why" is "I have coaching experience and knowledge that can help other introverts and help them be happier and more successful. I want to share that knowledge and help others."

- Talk to yourself in the third person. "Jennifer has got this. She is going to get this done well."

Figure 5.3: Speaking to yourself with compassion

Self-compassion is the act of forgiving ourselves when we are not perfect. It is a foundational building block in mental health, and we need to practice it consistently. Self-compassion is a particularly critical skill for introverts because we are prone to self-criticism (a topic I'll discuss further in Chapter 7).

Self-compassion is a practice that you should be doing for the rest of your life, whether it's related to work or not. Importantly, it is not a one and done; doing it once doesn't mean you don't need to do it again. Self-compassion is like mindfulness: It becomes easier over time. Also, don't be afraid that if you give yourself compassion, you will become lazy or not try to improve. You will be amazed that it actually works in reverse. You become stronger faster because you are not wasting all your time ruminating and beating yourself up. Accept yourself, especially as an introvert, and all of your idiosyncrasies, even if society is telling you differently. Try one small statement of self-compassion today.

Having an Inner Compass Guide Your Way

In this chapter, we began building awareness of your Inner Compass by using the four outer dimensions of the compass:

1. Allow your mind to settle with mindfulness.
2. Learn to pay attention to your intuition.
3. Identify your purpose and connect it with your day-to-day life, particularly at work.
4. Practice self-compassion daily—you will be happier and more accepting of yourself and others.

All of these tools will help you be your authentic self without changing who you are. They are ongoing actions you can practice to keep you true to yourself. Confidence is not out there. It is within you. In the next chapter, I'll talk about how to connect these four compass points so you can hear your Wisdom Within speaking to you.

CONFIDENCE IS NOT OUT THERE. IT IS WITHIN YOU.

ACTIONS TO CONSIDER

Strengthening your Inner Compass is one of the most effective ways for introverts to develop confidence in their actions. Start by thinking about the four outer dimensions of the compass: mindfulness, intuition, purpose, and self-compassion. Where do you feel strongest? Weakest? Choose one to start focusing on. Here are some suggestions in each area to get you started:

- Mindfulness: Focus on your senses (hearing, touch, sight, taste, smell) for five to ten minutes.
- Intuition: Listen to that inner knowing. Do some deep breathing if your intuition is not clear yet. Experiment with following your intuition in a low-risk situation, like what you want to do on the weekend. Then build confidence in using it at work in bigger decisions.
- Purpose: Think about a meeting you're going to attend in the near future. Do you know why you're going? What purpose can you fill in that meeting better than anyone else? If you want to start defining a broader purpose in life, use the Five Whys to dig down into what you are meant to do. Check out the suggested books mentioned in the chapter.
- Self-Compassion: If you start having negative thoughts about yourself, recognize the emotions you're feeling. Think about your common humanity and say words of encouragement to yourself.

If it helps, download the *Lead with Quiet Confidence Workbook* at www.JenniferMarcou.com/resources to help you to capture your thoughts on these and other exercises.

6

Connecting to the Wisdom Within

Nothing can dim the light that shines from within.
—Maya Angelou

We as introverts can spend a lot of our time pretending to act like extroverts, as that is what we think is expected of us. It may be difficult to stay grounded in who we really are, especially when we feel like our real self is not as acceptable or successful in this extroverted world. The key to confidence as an introvert is to find and be your authentic self, introverted characteristics and all, by connecting with what you know to be true.

I call this place the Wisdom Within. We all have it, a voice that is truly us. It is normally calm, confident, and clear. I know you have felt that voice in your life. Perhaps you felt it when you decided to accept a job or when you decided you wanted to be with your partner or when you just knew you wanted to go to a particular restaurant. It shows up at various times, yet it feels like we cannot always control when it will show up. Your Wisdom Within is your true self.

The elements we discussed in the previous chapter—mindfulness, intuition, purpose, and self-compassion—help us find our Wisdom Within place, where we can find the answers to how to approach challenges and be successful authentically ourselves, without changing who we are. Listening to your Wisdom Within's advice, you can be successful in managing your energy, networking, asking for a promotion, speaking up, presenting to large audiences, and much more. Your Wisdom Within fully embraces your introverted self and helps you be successful and continue to be you!

The challenge we all face—introverts and extroverts alike—is that it's not always easy to hear the voice of the Wisdom Within. Sometimes it is very quiet and hard to hear over all the other critical voices and busyness of life. Listening to our Wisdom Within means drawing on our mindfulness, allowing our intuition to shine through, and placing events in the context of our purpose (whether small *p* or big *P*). We need to practice self-compassion. And accessing your Wisdom Within allows you to connect more effectively with all four of these components.

Doing all of that becomes easier if we learn how to reduce all the other voices in our head and find our true voice, the voice that we are and we want to embrace. The most effective way I've discovered to make that happen is through visualization. In this chapter, I'll talk about what visualization is and how it can help us connect to our Wisdom Within.

WISDOM WITHIN BY ANY OTHER NAME

There are many different names for what I call Wisdom Within. In *Playing Big*, Tara Mohr calls it your "Inner Mentor" in addition to "Inner Wisdom." Shirzad Chamine in *Positive Intelligence* calls it your "Elder Wiser Self" or your "Sage." My coaching instructor and mentor, Patty Burgin of SeattleCoach, explained it in terms of living in the future and identifying who we are going to be thanking for our success.

The Wisdom Within Visualization Exercise

As the name implies, visualization is the act of picturing in your mind some future version of yourself, including things you do and don't want in your life, how you attained a goal, what your life is like when you attain that goal, and so on.

According to Richard Restak, MD, author of *The Naked Brain*, the research of Duke University psychologist Tanya L. Chartrand shows that thinking about something and doing it are neurologically similar, activating the same regions of the brain. As a result, imagining a desired state can be the first step toward self-improvement. For instance, you can envision yourself as the person you want to become or change a situation that's troubling you by imagining that change as a prelude to making it happen.

I've found that visualization exercises are particularly helpful for introverts who want to be leaders because it allows them to envision themselves as successful leaders (without having to become an extrovert) and imagine what that would look like and what it might take to get there. The Wisdom Within exercise is a visualization of yourself as that future successful leader.

The specific Wisdom Within visualization I developed takes about twenty minutes of uninterrupted time. Detailed instructions will be at the end of this chapter, but here is an overview of the structure:

- The exercise starts with a mindfulness body scan exercise I learned when I was young. This component is critical for bringing you into a space to leave behind anything else you're thinking about.
- The second stage is walking up the steps of a rainbow-colored staircase that leads you up into the clouds and space. This segment helps create a big-picture mindset where you feel awe and realize you are a component of a broader universe.
- As you return to Earth, you are asked to visit yourself twenty years into the future and think about what is important to that person and what advice they would give the current you.

Afterward, you are asked to write down as much detail as you can about what you saw and felt in that future experience. While this exercise can be helpful for everyone, introverts find it particularly helpful as a way to guide their inner reflections and resulting external actions, despite what competing internal and external forces say.

It seems strange to say that my intuition influences my life, but without conscious effort, we don't always hear that inner voice. The Wisdom Within allows us to externalize that part of our brain, so we can truly listen to it. For many of my coaching clients, the Wisdom Within exercise is a powerful exercise and one they return to frequently. Tapping into their Wisdom Within brings them confidence and calmness to face any obstacle. Lack of confidence can hold an introvert back, but finding your true inner self can help you find that confidence that always exists inside of you. As you will see later in two client stories, their Wisdom Within helped them be more confident to share their ideas and to regain their energy after work.

Why Does the Wisdom Within Visualization Work?

Research has shown that if you connect with the version of yourself twenty years into the future, you will be more likely to take care of yourself and save more money. So connecting to your Wisdom Within can help you feel more confident today and start habits that will pay off in years to come.

Once you have had an experience connecting with your Wisdom Within, you may find it surprising and astonishing that you already have this voice inside of you, yet you may not have paid attention.

How does this exercise work? As we have discussed, there are many parts of our brain and many voices vying for attention. It is not surprising that we don't focus in on this cool, calm, confident one. Our brains are designed to keep us alive, not to feel happy or fulfilled. If you are alive right now, the brain says, "Great—keep doing what you are doing."

Any change creates a risk from the brain's perspective that you may not be alive after that change. Our brain pays more attention to the negative emotions, as it wants to mitigate any risk. The introverted brain is a particular expert at rumination, so we can get stuck in negative emotions. The positive emotions—or perspective that the Wisdom Within provides—are underplayed in our minds, particularly in times of stress. Connecting regularly and explicitly to your Wisdom Within is a way to focus the brain on that intuitive, confident, true voice that is within us all.

ALTERNATE EXERCISE: WILL THIS MATTER IN TWENTY YEARS?

If this visualization exercise I describe here doesn't resonate with you, just let it go. Many people are not able to visualize, and that is completely OK. Another way to get to a similar insight is to ask yourself whether whatever challenge you are facing will matter in twenty years. You can usually get a quick response to that question.

For example, ask yourself, *Will the stress I am feeling about tomorrow's sales call matter in twenty years?* I bet the answer is a quick no. But perhaps what matters is whether you are able to overcome that anxiety to do sales or realize that perhaps this sales role is not for you. Usually, it becomes very clear when you ask yourself whether something will matter in twenty years—either it won't or you will identify what will matter.

Using Your Wisdom Within in Day-to-Day Life

The insights you gain and lessons learned from completing a Wisdom Within visualization exercise can help you outside of doing the exercise. For example, when I was naming my coaching business, I asked my Wisdom Within, whom I'd named Daphne, what she thought. She said people will hire me for me, not the business name, so the business name did not matter as much as I worried it did. That is how I arrived at the simple Marcou Coaching name. I can (and do) thank Daphne for that and a myriad of other advice. She has been a key influence on my life, whether that's in making a decision or feeling more confident in my decision.

Here are three practical ways to reconnect with your future self and use it to guide your decisions and choices in the present day.

1. Revisit Your Wisdom Within

Go through the Wisdom Within visualization again. Or just find a quiet space, close your eyes, take a few deep breaths, and imagine you are on the doorstep of the place where your future self or Wisdom Within lives. Ask any question you want, from big life decisions to what you want to have for dinner. Your future self will answer you with words or a sign. Whatever your interpretation, it is correct, since your Wisdom Within is your visualization of your future self. It is you.

Take Sabrina, for example. She is a director of partnerships for a global luxury goods company and was nervous in front of senior leaders in meetings. Her boss was highly extroverted and was always speaking. Her skip level (boss's boss) was an expert in the industry. Sabrina was hesitant to say anything in meetings in front of her skip level in case she showed her lack of knowledge or was uncomfortable interrupting her loquacious boss, so her good ideas were not coming out. She was worried that her leaders did not think she had new ideas. Every meeting she did not speak up, she felt she'd failed. And when she did try to share an idea, her boss would interrupt her. She was frustrated and felt like giving up.

After going through the Wisdom Within exercise in our coaching session, she now had a new tool to inspire her to share her ideas in meetings. Before a particularly important meeting on annual planning and budgeting, she revisited her Wisdom Within and realized she could bring that internal confidence by holding her hands together in her lap just like her Wisdom Within would do. When she felt reticent to speak up, she held her hands together and felt the energy and confidence of her Wisdom Within.

One idea she suggested (while holding her hands together!) was, "Why don't we tier the investments we make in partnerships by impact to our brand instead of sales?" It was an idea she had been noodling on for a couple of weeks. Her boss thought it was a great idea and came up with even more ideas building on Sabrina's suggestion. Her skip level said that it was a very innovative idea, as everyone was always pushing on tying investment to sales, but with partnerships it makes it much more difficult to do. Sabrina was a hero in the meeting.

Her palms were sweaty, but they were still in the strong symbolic position of being held together, channeling her Wisdom Within throughout the conversation. She said the Wisdom Within handhold was a game changer in not only how she felt in the moment of a stressor but also in helping her prepare, as she knew her Wisdom Within would always be there for her with just a touch of her hands. She knew she could be ready for anything with a more confident and calm presence.

2. Channel Your Wisdom Within—Ask What Your Future Self Would Do in a Situation

If you have a difficult decision coming up or a stressful presentation, you can ask what your Wisdom Within would do. It is helpful to use the name, which is different from your current name, so you can differentiate that voice inside of you.

Usually, clients are able to respond very quickly to the question, "What would your Wisdom Within do if they were in your situation?" even though they may be hemming and hawing about what to do.

Imagining your future self as a second party allows you to pull out the best part of you and embody that. It represents compassion and encouragement without judgment. It is not worried about perfection or what others think. It is part of your subconscious mind that can help you see a future. Your Wisdom Within's perspective is not comingled with other perceptions you may have of yourself. It can give you confidence and direction in life. Importantly, you do not have to do what your Wisdom Within says. But you are getting a clear perspective from your intuition that you can evaluate as you decide what to do.

3. Emulate Your Wisdom Within

The third way to connect with your Wisdom Within is to emulate them. Think about what your Wisdom Within would do if your future self had an hour on a weekend free. Would your future self read? Go for a hike? Garden? Go to a museum? Take an art class? Whatever it is, try it next weekend. If it is something you already do today, when you do that activity, actively state to yourself that you are doing this activity because your Wisdom Within does this.

Think about what your Wisdom Within would do for a Saturday night dinner. Would your Wisdom Within have a quiet night at home ordering delivery, make a new recipe for family and friends, or go out to a restaurant? Identify specifically what kind of food your future self would eat and with whom. Then plan a meal like that and again connect that activity to the fact that your Wisdom Within would do this.

You can even open up your closet one day and wear what your Wisdom Within would select from your wardrobe.

The key is to start doing the things your Wisdom Within does, but do them now instead of waiting for twenty years. You are becoming your Wisdom Within sooner. Your future self is you!

For example, Ginny was spending a lot of energy having negative thoughts about herself and others. She felt like she was not a good employee, as she had to get home early to pick up her kids from after-school activities. And she felt like she was not a good wife and mother, as she was so tired at dinner and did not actively engage in conversations with her family about their days. She was stressed about her role as an engineer on a new product launch. The project was delayed due to quality assurance, and she was not sure how to move it forward. She had a short temper at work with her colleagues. That stress made it difficult for her to be present with her family.

After the Wisdom Within visualization, she imagined what her best self would do in certain situations. The gift her Wisdom Within gave her was a flowered apron like the kind her grandma used to wear. She felt this represented love and putting her family first. She bought an apron in real life and her whole family noticed and loved it. At the same time, that negative energy started to shift. She had more patience with others and especially with herself. She gave herself more self-compassion.

When quality assurance would not respond to her emails, she would try showing up in their offices. She raised the issue to her boss. She was calm and methodical in her approach versus focusing on feelings of frustration. And most importantly, she gave herself grace realizing she was doing the best she could. In that calmer state, she was able to creatively brainstorm with her boss on how to move through the blockage by soliciting more quality assurance resources.

Because she had calmed her feeling of stress at work, she now had more energy to spend with her family when she got home at night. She recognized the emotions she was having, letting them go and seeing the positive especially in conserving her energy to focus on what was important—her family. She wondered why she had spent so much time worrying about the perception her boss may have by letting him know about the quality assurance problems. She realized those negative emotions were not important. That apron was a visual representation of the fact that her Wisdom Within was with her all along, reminding Ginny to focus on the important things like family and letting the small stuff go.

Use Your Wisdom Within

The Wisdom Within visualization is a powerful tool to keep you connected to your authentic self. It is your best self, your intuition, your true self. It is what will give you the confidence to be yourself but in ways that allow you to achieve your goals.

There are a variety of ways to keep connected to your Wisdom Within. Referring to your Wisdom Within can help you be more confident, change your mindset, and make decisions. It can also help you prepare *before* a stressful situation as well as have the confident presence you want to have in the moment. For example, like Sabrina, you can channel your Wisdom Within before you go into a stressful situation. She created a physical connection to her Wisdom Within by holding her hands together. You could take five minutes before the situation and visualize how your Wisdom Within would show up in that meeting.

Personally, I revisit mine when I have a difficult decision to make, or if I don't have a lot of time, I channel her, asking myself what she would do in my situation. I have even picked up drawing, even though I don't consider myself artistic, because my Wisdom Within is an artist. You can find a Wisdom Within strategy that works for you, even if it is simply asking yourself whether what is challenging you will matter in twenty years.

Connecting to your Wisdom Within can allow you to identify your true self, including your introverted preferences, and intuitively identify ways for you to show up and act to be successful. Your Wisdom Within will stop you from acting like an extrovert and will help you find ways to be successful without changing who you are in your soul. Whether it is making decisions to attend (or not) events that exhaust you or volunteering to present to large audiences, your Wisdom Within can guide you in the goals that you have for yourself.

Instructions for the Wisdom Within Visualization Exercise

Make sure you have twenty minutes of uninterrupted time so you can ponder and journal afterward. Find a quiet location where you can sit comfortably. Turn off your phone and all distractions. Make sure you have paper and a pen to jot down your thoughts afterward. Get comfy.

TIP: Because reading this at the same time as doing the visualization may be challenging, it is best to listen to it. Please visit www.JenniferMarcou.com/resources to download the recording.

Another option is to record yourself reading this, or have someone else read it to you, and then listen to the recording to do the exercise.

Close your eyes. Put your feet flat on the floor. Rest your hands loosely in your lap.

Take three deep breaths—in through your nose for four counts, out through your mouth 2—3—4.

Breathe in through your nose 2—3—4. Out through your mouth 2—3—4.

Breathe in through your nose 2—3—4. Out through your mouth 2—3—4.

Now just return to normal breathing. Notice the rising and falling of your chest as you breathe normally.

Imagine your body is floating in a cool, calm lake. Feel the current moving softly against your skin.

Focus your attention on your feet. Notice any tension or stress in your feet—let it go. Let all the tension and stress flow out of your feet into the cool water.

Move your attention upward to your ankles and your calves. Relax your muscles and tendons. Let any tension or stress flow out of this area.

Next focus on your knees. Let any tension or stress release from the front and the back of the knees. Move your attention upward to your thighs—your quads and hamstrings. Relax your upper legs—letting any tension float out and into the cool lake.

Now focus on your pelvic area, relaxing your hips. With a breath in, let your belly fully expand, and a breath out, let your belly fully release.

Move your attention to your lower back, your middle back, your upper back. Let all the tension and stress flow down your back and out into the cool water.

Now focus on your upper arms. Relax your biceps and your triceps. Soften your elbows. Relax your lower arms. Let all the tension flow down to your hands and out through your fingertips into the cool water.

Now relax your shoulders. Maybe do some shoulder rolls forward, then backward. Relax your neck. Maybe do a neck roll to one side, then the other.

Soften your jaw. Relax your lips. Release your tongue from the roof of your mouth. Relax your cheeks. Relax all the little muscles around your eyes. Soften your brow. Relax your forehead. Relax your scalp.

Now imagine a colorful stairway made of all the colors of the rainbow.

Move to the first step, up onto the red step. You are completely encased in the color red. Soak in the rich red color. Feel the temperature of the color for a moment.

Now move onto the next step, to the orange. Feel the orange color penetrating your skin. Notice what your body feels like.

Move onto the next step, up to the yellow. What do you feel when you are surrounded by yellow? What taste do you imagine? What smell do you imagine?

Now move up to the green step. How does the green make you feel? Take a deep breath in and notice what your lungs feel. Let it out.

Now move onto the next blue step. What does the blue remind you of? What emotion do you feel when you see the blue all around you? Take a moment to take it all in.

Move up to the indigo step. What do you notice with your eyes as you are surrounded by indigo? What does it feel like?

Now move to the violet step. What are you noticing about the violet color? What does it remind you of?

Now the staircase continues, but the steps are completely white. Continue moving up the stairs into the sky. And soon, you are going up so high into the sky that you are moving through the clouds. Earth is getting smaller and smaller. Soon you are in space. Dark, blue, and black. You can see the planets and the stars. And you keep moving out into the dark vastness of space.

You see a big comfy cloud in front of you. Sit down into that big fluffy cloud, which perfectly holds your weight and feels like it was meant to fit your body. You can see the little ball of Earth, like the size of a marble. You can see the Milky Way with millions of stars sparkling.

Just be with yourself for a moment. There is nowhere else you are meant to be in this moment. Take a deep breath and sink into the cloud a little more. Take one more deep breath and let it out.

Now you realize it is time to get back to Earth. Start floating back toward Earth on the big fluffy cloud. As you get closer, notice what part of the world you are coming to. You realize you are going to visit your future self, yourself twenty years from now.

Earth is getting closer. You can see the blue of the oceans and the brown, green, and white of the land. As you get closer to Earth, you realize you are going to the home of your future self. The cloud lets you off right at the front door of the home of your future self, yourself in twenty years.

Notice where your future self lives. Take a look around. What does the home look like? What does the landscaping look like? What does it feel like to be here?

As you knock on the door, your future self in twenty years opens the door and welcomes you in. Take in their presence. What words would you use to describe them? How do you feel in their presence? What are they wearing?

You notice the inside of the house. They take you to their favorite part of the house for a chat. Notice what it feels like to be in their special space. You sit down to talk. You have lots of questions.

Ask them, "What has mattered most in the past twenty years?"

Listen to their answer. They won't always answer with words, but it may be a symbol or image or feeling. Just notice what they say or what is coming up for you if they respond without words. "What has mattered most in the past twenty years?"

Ask, "What is important for me to know right now?"

Again, let them respond in any way they are able. If there are no words, that is OK. Just notice how you are feeling. "What is important for me to know right now?"

Ask, "What advice do you have for me?" Mentally record whatever they say or share in their facial or body language. "What advice do you have for me?"

Now ask them about a problem or dilemma you are facing. It could be something at work or in your personal life, big or small. Ask their perspective. What advice do they have? What would they do?

Finally, ask them, "What is your name?" What do they want to be called? The name may make sense to you or it may not.

Now thank your future self for their advice and guidance. As you are getting ready to leave, they bring a gift to you. Open up that gift.

Now go back to the place where the cloud dropped you off. It is there waiting for you. Jump on the comfy, cushy cloud and begin to move up into the sky. Notice their house getting smaller as you go higher and higher into space. Notice the white stairs and then the color stairs where you started. Float down the rainbow stairs until you get to the chair where you started this experience.

Come back into the present. Feel your body against the chair. Feel your feet against the floor. Wiggle your toes. Wiggle your fingers. Slowly open your eyes.

Debrief: What Did You See and Feel?

Now take a few minutes to jot down some notes about what you experienced. You can journal about where your future self lived and what it felt like to be in their presence. Note any answers to the questions you asked them. You can also look at the reflection questions for more details.

- What has mattered most in the past twenty years?
- What is important for me to know right now?
- What advice do they have for me?

- What is their name?
- What was the gift they gave you?

Write as much detail as you can about what you saw. No detail is too small to mention. For whatever reason, your brain came up with all these details, so it is important to capture them. Then write about what you felt in the experience. Reflect on the guidance and wisdom you received.

If your future self gave you the same name as your name now or you were not given a name, decide how you want to refer to your future self. Sometimes my coaching clients use an adjective for the name, such as Calm, Confidence, or Peaceful. Sometimes the name is a personal nickname people had for them when they were little. Sometimes it is a completely new, unfamiliar name, with no logical origin. Look up the name to see if it means anything, if that is the case. Sometimes people just want to call it their Wisdom Within, or as Tara Mohr would call it, your Inner Mentor, or as Shirzad Chamine would call it, your Sage. Make sure you refer to it with a different name from you in the present day.

Research shows if you speak to yourself in the third person, you will use more positive language. That is why it is important to name your Wisdom Within something different from your name so that you can talk about your Wisdom Within in the third person. My Wisdom Within is named Daphne. So I say things like, "Daphne will show up in tomorrow's meeting confident and calm and will be OK if she does not know all the answers." This third-person statement is more effective at changing my mindset than saying simply, "I will show up confident." That last statement does not sound believable to me, and my critical negative voice (about which we will learn more in the next chapter) tells me all the reasons I will not be confident.

Some people may worry that they see only their Wisdom Within and not other people, like a partner, family, or pets. This does not mean you will be alone in the future. This visualization is purely about yourself, so the brain focuses only on you. In all my years of doing this in my coaching, I have had only one client imagine a second person in their visualization. It is OK to be alone in the visualization; it is not a prediction of the future.

What If You Did Not See Much in the Visualization Experience?

If the visualization did not work for you, that is completely valid. It may not be the right place or time. Everyone's brains work differently, and visualizations may not work for you. If this was not a meaningful experience or instructive exercise, here are some tips:

- **Identify any details you did see.** Some details—such as, for example, a red front door—may not seem relevant. Others may make sense if you think about it over time. For example, perhaps your grandmother had a red door, and you felt safe at her house. Other details may make no sense to you now but may make sense over time—or not. For some reason, your brain came up with these details. Contemplate what they mean to you.
- **Focus on the feelings you had.** What did it feel like to be at the house in the presence of your future self? Did you feel calm, welcome, safe?
    - If you felt negative emotions, this may not have been the right place or right time for this exercise. Try again another time. If the negative emotions are too overwhelming, please reach out to a mental health professional for support.
- **Try the visualization at another time.** Identify a time when you are calm and able to focus on the exercise. If you do this exercise multiple times, don't be concerned if the details change. That

is normal, because your mindset is different each time you go through the exercise.

- **Contemplate the questions and consider how your future self would answer.** Even if you did not hear anything from your future self during the exercise, you can still think about what your future self might do or say.

ACTIONS TO CONSIDER

- Complete the Wisdom Within visualization exercise or the "will this matter in twenty years?" exercise.
- Consider ways to reconnect with your Wisdom Within periodically:
  - Revisit your Wisdom Within by going through the visualization again.
  - Channel the voice of your Wisdom Within.
  - Emulate your future self.
- Create a Kind goal to experiment with one of the Wisdom Within strategies. Select a time and place to try that strategy.

Remember to download the *Lead with Quiet Confidence Workbook* at www.JenniferMarcou.com/resources to help you to capture your thoughts on your Wisdom Within visualization and reflect on how to use it to feel more confident.

7

Tuning Out Your Critical Voice

The more you practice self-acceptance,
the more you'll realize the only person
whose acceptance you ever needed is your own.
—Mel Robbins

I spent the first twenty years of my career in financial services, never asking for a promotion or negotiating a salary. I thought my good work (competence) would be recognized. But really, I was nervous that I would embarrass myself. I had an inner voice that would say things like, *Who am I to ask for a promotion? I am not very good at negotiating. Maybe I don't create that much value. I don't deserve a higher salary. If they really valued me, they would promote me without me asking. I am going to embarrass myself. Maybe they will fire me or rescind my offer.*

But as I matured in my career, I realized that I had to get over myself. Other people were successfully asking for promotions. Other people were successfully negotiating their salaries. My lack of confidence in my worth to my company was putting me at a disadvantage. When I got the offer at Microsoft before starting my own business, I realized the pain of negotiating the salary would be much smaller than the longer-term impact of a higher salary. I realized my purpose in the offer negotiation was to get what I was worth and to benefit my family. I prepared for the negotiation in part by silencing that inner critical voice: Whenever I had a negative thought about my ability to successfully negotiate, I would remind myself that I was doing it for my family. I built up my confidence by focusing on my family.

Guess what? I did negotiate. The HR person really pushed back on the terms I wanted, and I didn't get everything I asked for, but I got more than the original offer.

It took me way too long in my career to get to this point of overcoming my fears. I think about what opportunities and income I lost without negotiating all those years—what I lost by letting what I now call my Critical Voice take the lead and not my Wisdom Within.

In this chapter, we'll explore that negative voice in our head that tells us that we are not good enough or smart enough or outgoing enough or extroverted enough, the voice that says we can't do what we aspire to do. I'll also talk about practical strategies for learning how to tune out that voice, even if just temporarily. My hope is that these strategies will expedite your learning and help you empower yourself more quickly than I did by reducing negative and self-limiting thoughts.

Critical Voices Are Harsh

The Critical Voice is the one that tells us we are not good enough or we are not ready. It erodes our confidence by making us doubt our skills, our thoughts, our wisdom. It can be a broken record or a tape that keeps playing.

One of my clients, Nate, was a senior manager at a large financial services company. Despite his title, he was very uncomfortable sending emails to more senior leaders, aside from his boss. Nate's Critical Voice was having a field day, suggesting that the recipient senior leader would realize he was wrong or not as smart as originally thought. No wonder he would reread the email several times before sending, fearful that there was going to be something wrong in it. And even after he finally did hit send on an email, he continued to reread the email, predicting what negative reaction the recipient would have.

I have felt like this many times, even as a senior leader. One lesson from my and Nate's experience is that the level of seniority does not matter. That darn Critical Voice can buzz in any introvert's brain, magnifying the potential risk of whatever action is being contemplated, be it asking for a promotion or sending an email. I have coached many introverts who have the same issue—worrying about how people will react and particularly worrying that somehow people will find out they are not as good as they once thought.

Welcome to your Critical Voice. It comes from self-doubt. It is harsh; it says things to us that we would never say to someone else. It usually comes out when we have low energy or are stressed or are out of our comfort zone, which may be common states for introverts.

NEGATIVITY IS A REFLEX. CONFIDENCE IS A PRACTICE.

To be clear, all healthy humans have a negative internal voice. It's linked to a part of the brain that is afraid, that wants to keep you safe, and in that way, it plays an important role. If your Critical Voice is showing up, pay attention to it. Don't ignore it or try to bury it. Understand what it is afraid of and try to reduce its impact. But just don't wallow in it. Negativity is a reflex. Confidence is a practice.

Our brain defaults to negative stories so it can protect us. Even in this modern world, where we do not have tigers around to hunt us, our mind treats negative feedback, disapproval, even a weird look as dangerous. Our body increases adrenaline to prepare for a fight-or-flight response and creates cortisol from stress.

The extra challenge for introverts is, because we are so in our heads, we tend to ruminate on those negative feelings. And unfortunately, that rumination usually zeroes in on something negative we are saying about ourselves to ourselves. Perhaps it is the presentation you did yesterday when you forgot to make an important point—how stupid of you. Perhaps it is the typo in the email you just sent to senior leaders—how careless. You get the picture.

CRITICS, SABOTEURS, AND JUDGES

You may already be familiar with what I'm calling the Critical Voice if you've read *Playing Big* by Tara Mohr, who calls it the Inner Critic. Or *Positive Intelligence*, where author Shirzad Chamine calls it our saboteurs or, specifically, the judge of ourselves. Jill Bolte Taylor calls it Character 2 of your brain, the part that is fearful and tries to keep you safe. Patty Burgin of SeattleCoach calls it the critical voices. However you label it, it is harsh, negative, and repetitive.

Critical Voice Versus Wisdom Within

I used to think I needed an internal critical voice because it made me work harder and therefore become better. It pointed out all my errors. How could I improve if I didn't know the mistakes I made?

But eventually I came to a different realization. Have you ever had a horrible boss, teacher, or parent tell you that you are wrong, but at the same time they did not help you understand how to improve? Compare that to a great boss, teacher, or parent who helps coach you by giving you feedback and helping you improve going forward and making you feel good about the growth. Which scenario would you prefer? The horrible boss is your Critical Voice, always criticizing but not actually helping you to improve. Obviously, having a great boss is not only much more pleasant, but you are more likely to grow from it.

Let me give you an example. Let's say I had presented to a group yesterday and it did not go so well. People seemed to be falling asleep or leaving the room.

My Critical Voice would say, *You did a horrible job of presenting. You are* always *a horrible presenter*. Notice how my Critical Voice is giving me harsh feedback but not providing any ideas on how to improve? And not only is it giving me negative feedback, but it is generalizing that I am "always" a horrible presenter. That is not necessarily true. How is this helpful?

The voice of my Wisdom Within, on the other hand, speaks from self-compassion. It helps you build your confidence, not undermine it. It would say, *The presentation did not go as well as you expected. You did a good job at sharing your subject-matter expertise. However, the audience was not engaged. Perhaps next time you could tell a story to engage your audience more.*

That is helpful! My Wisdom Within recognized the facts, understood what I did well, and, most importantly, gave me advice about what I could do better next time. This is feed*forward*, not feed*back*. It helps my performance going forward much more than the Critical Voice.

To improve, you need your Wisdom Within, not your Critical Voice. Your Wisdom Within is honest, compassionate, and helpful, whereas your Critical Voice can be brutal, harsh, and unproductive.

You will know when your Critical Voice is speaking because it will be negative and make you feel bad. It feeds on your insecurities. It is binary—either right or wrong. There is no gray or nuance. It is reactive and focuses on problems, not solutions. And it can be very repetitive. It focuses on the past and is worried about the future. It is rarely in the present. It can feel like you are stuck and alone.

On the other hand, your Wisdom Within is positive, or at least neutral. It is solution-oriented and is focused on forward movement, not wallowing in the past. It is proactive and helps you deal with the present moment. It is calm and curious. It sees possibilities. The Wisdom Within is "we" focused, not "me" focused. It wants to connect with others.

How can you dampen or silence your Critical Voice and make room for your Wisdom Within to make an appearance? I like to start with the visualization exercise at the end of this chapter.

Silencing a Critical Voice

I've developed a Critical Voice visualization exercise with influences from Tara Mohr's Inner Critic framework and Dr. Jill Bolte Taylor's four characters of the brain. The visualization helps people learn to recognize and conquer their negative narrator. You can find the full instructions at the end of this chapter, but the idea is to develop a persona for your Critical Voice so you can deal with it just as you would another person. Here's a quick overview of the exercise:

1. It starts with a few minutes of deep breathing designed to calm your brain and improve mindfulness.
2. Then I ask you to think about *when* your Critical Voice most often appears and what it says. This will help you learn to anticipate the voice and be proactive in disarming it.

3. In the third segment, I invite you to visualize your Critical Voice as a real person or a character from a book or movie, and even give it a name if you want. (Mine is named Larry.) I have you ask questions of this persona and inquire into issues like what its motivations are and how it's helped you in the past.
4. In the fourth segment, you define new activities that this Critical Voice persona can do that don't involve criticizing you, and imagine scenarios where you expect it to appear but can direct it toward these other activities.

Let me share a story of how one of my clients used this exercise to help silence her Critical Voice.

Sheri Sends "Miranda" to a Paris Fashion Show

When completing the above exercise, Sheri, a project manager for an advertising company, personified her Critical Voice as Miranda from *The Devil Wears Prada*, the ruthless boss of the movie's heroine. Miranda was critical of Sheri when she had ideas to solve a problem at work. She was harsh and unrelenting. *Who are you to think of new ideas? You don't have enough experience. You are not smart enough. No one is going to listen to you.*

Sheri realized that because she'd been listening to Miranda, she'd held herself back from sharing her ideas, even though in her heart she thought they could be helpful. Once we went through the Critical Voice exercise, Sheri realized she would get butterflies in her stomach when she started feeling self-doubt. That was her early warning sign that Miranda was about to appear. So she would preemptively send Miranda to Fashion Week while Sheri shared her ideas with her team on how to work more efficiently.

Suddenly, Miranda's voice was a lot quieter. No longer was she driving, or rather backseat driving; she wasn't even in the car.

Over time, Sheri identified the situations where Miranda was most likely to show up, like high-stakes contentious discussions or in meetings with senior leaders. She could plan ahead of time to send Miranda away. And if Miranda did show up, Sheri would remind her to get back to Paris before she missed the next Prada runway show. Sheri felt freer to be herself, and she was rewarded for her higher performance with a great bonus that year. She stopped limiting herself.

Three Approaches for Dimming a Critical Voice

The Critical Voice visualization exercise incorporates three techniques for dealing with that voice: naming and personifying it, asking it to be helpful rather than just critical, and sending it off to Paris (or any other locale that's not where you are!). These techniques fall into three general approaches labeled the 3Rs (see Figure 7.1).

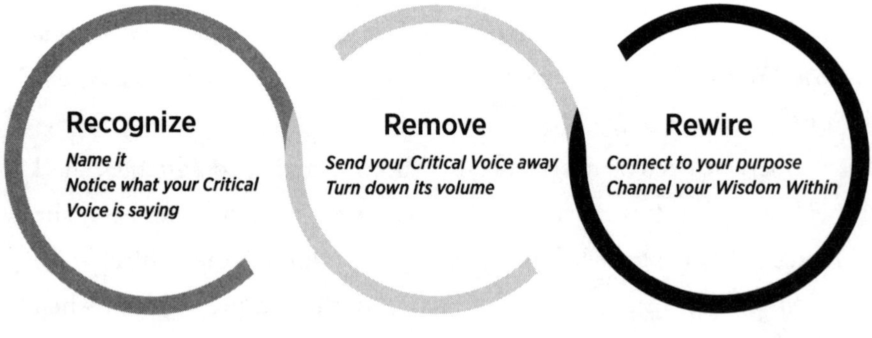

Figure 7.1: The 3Rs for silencing a Critical Voice

1. **Recognize** your Critical Voice is there.
2. **Remove** your Critical Voice from the scene.
3. **Rewire** by shifting your perspective from your Critical Voice to your Wisdom Within and purpose.

Let's go through the strategies in each bucket.

1. Recognize Your Critical Voice Is There

The first essential ingredient for dealing with a Critical Voice is to simply recognize when it is present and give it a personality (mine is named Larry). Here are some actions that fit this category (some of which you'll recognize from the visualization exercise):

- **Create a character of your Critical Voice.** Sometimes just recognizing it is there can help.
- **Notice and label the Critical Voice.** Call them by name—*Here comes Larry again.*
- **Recognize the Critical Voice's role is to keep you safe.** Don't get mad at it. Be curious about the role it wants to play in your life. *Larry, what purpose are you serving here?*
- **Look for the humor in what your Critical Voice is saying.** Be playful. *Larry is a worry wart. The sky is not falling, Larry.*
- **Take your Critical Voice's concern to the extreme to see how irrational it can be.** *I'm going to be fired, then I will lose my house, I will lose my family, and I will be living on the street eating cat food.*

Sometimes it is as simple as just recognizing that your Critical Voice is there to minimize its impact on you.

2. Remove Your Critical Voice from the Scene

Just as Sheri did with Miranda, think of a creative way to get the voice out of your head. Here are some typical options:

- **Send your Critical Voice to its favorite activity.** *Larry, it is time to go hiking.*
- **Imagine the Critical Voice receding into space.** Keep moving it farther and farther away until there is no air and you cannot hear what it says.
- **Imagine turning down the volume on the Critical Voice.** Give your Critical Voice a volume control and dial it down to a 1 or even a 0.
- **Visualize placing all the negative in a basket.** And then, most importantly, move that basket outside your office, maybe even outside the door of the building you are in. Your concerns will be there when you are done. But it has to stay out of the room while you make that decision or during that stressful meeting.

3. Rewire by Shifting Your Perspective to Your Wisdom Within

In the final set of strategies, you define a helpful role for your Critical Voice, asking it to think more like your Wisdom Within. Here are several examples of how to do this:

- **Ask your Critical Voice if it would play a different role.** *Larry, will you help me feel more confident (or "calm down" or "be present") instead of yelling at me or telling me I can't do this?*
- **Ask what your Wisdom Within would do.** What would they do and how would they feel if faced with this same challenge or decision?

- **Get curious about what you are afraid of.** Ask yourself what you are afraid of when your Critical Voice shows up.
- **Take an action that will put you into "flow."** Mihaly Csikszentmihalyi, a noted psychologist and a founder of positive psychology, defined "flow" as a state of optimal experience in which one's skills match the challenges of a situation. Specifically, "[f]low is being completely involved in an activity for its own sake. The ego falls away. Time flies. Every action, movement, and thought follows inevitably from the previous one, like playing jazz." The negative self-talk reduces when we're in flow. There is no room for the Critical Voice. Think of an activity that puts you into flow—for me, it is researching or learning or working on a tracking spreadsheet or any analysis project. I am relaxed and engaged and lose track of time. And my Critical Voice is quiet. When you reach that flow state, move back to the activity that was triggering your Critical Voice. Your mind should be calmer and the Critical Voice quieter.
- **Revisit the purpose or value you are serving** by taking the action you are taking (or decision you are making). *Larry, I have a unique perspective to add to this meeting, and it's important my ideas be heard.* For example, while writing this book, my Critical Voice, Larry, was saying to me, *Do I have enough to say to write a whole book? Will anyone value it? Who am I to write a book?* In response, I focused on my calling: my Purpose to help introverted professionals—all of you—build confidence, presence, and success. That reduced the negative questions and anxiety. It made Larry quiet down.

YOUR WHY IS STRONGER THAN YOUR WORRY.

YOUR WHY IS STRONGER THAN YOUR WORRY

Sanka was tongue-tied whenever she was asked at a conference what she liked to do for fun. She was not sure how to answer, and her Critical Voice, which she calls "the Emperor," made her tongue-tied. She realized she was afraid she would not sound interesting. When she realized the conversation was not about her fear but rather finding common ground to get to know a person, that fear became less important. She connected to her purpose, which was to meet people and learn about them. So she would pick something she would enjoy talking about, like reading books. Usually the other person enjoyed books, and they would have a good conversation. She would usually walk away with a new book recommendation. Connecting to your purpose, suddenly that Critical Voice quiets.

Think about which of these strategies resonates with you more and which ones you want to experiment with. Don't feel like you have to try all of them. Just pick one or two and try it out. If one does not work, try it again or try another one.

Changing Your Reactions to Negative Events

Sometimes, our negative thoughts are linked to real events, not just the fears in our head. A boyfriend or girlfriend breaks up with us, we lose a job, we lose a friend. In the moment, these experiences feel bad, and our Critical Voice may try to blame us. Or we may simply wallow in our misery. In addition to the strategies outlined previously to reduce your Critical Voice, there are more strategies to reduce negative emotions. Remember that negativity is a reflex; confidence is a practice. The brain has plasticity, the ability to change, so we can rewire negative habitual thoughts. Here are four strategies to reduce negative emotions:

1. **Identify the gift.** When something bad happens, you can always find the silver lining, something good that would have never happened if the "bad" thing did not happen. For example, the job you lost led you to the job you now have and love. Every situation can turn into a gift. It is identifying the good that could come of something. According to Shirzad Chamine of *Positive Intelligence*, if a bad situation happens, "accept or convert it." Accept the situation without negative feeling or if you cannot, then convert it to a gift, something good.
2. **Reframe the situation.** Have you ever been to a meeting and a colleague leaves that meeting with a very different perspective than you do? And you were at the same meeting! It makes you realize there are so many different ways to think. You can leverage that idea by actively reframing situations to see a different perspective. For example, instead of feeling frustrated stuck in traffic, recognize you have time to think through tomorrow's agenda. Next time you are in a dilemma and feel there are no solutions, think of ways to reframe the situation to come up with new solutions.
3. **Show gratitude.** Another way to deal with negative situations or mindsets is to acknowledge your gratitude. I know a fellow coach, Katherine, whose workplace requires her to have more coaching calls a day than she has energy for. She writes in a gratitude journal every day, and this practice of gratitude allows her to switch from rumination on what she is upset about to what she is grateful for—which is to do what she loves (coaching). She is always the first person to point out that she is so grateful for her husband, her family, and to do the work she loves, even in the face of challenges and frustrations. Whatever it is, being grateful allows you to realize you likely have an abundance of things to be happy about.

4. **Take one small step forward.** Brain science shows that taking one step forward allows us to get out of our ruts. So to get out of negative thinking and rumination on a bad situation, take one small step forward. Susan, a microbiologist at a biotech firm, was planning for her maternity leave four months away and was procrastinating starting a difficult project. She felt guilty about her lack of action, and her Critical Voice would kick in, making her feel anxious and overwhelmed. In our coaching discussion on her priorities before her leave, she realized this project was an important one she knew she wanted to finish. She finally identified that on the following Monday, she would cancel her meetings and dedicate the afternoon to starting the project. That one small step led to others, and she felt rewarded for her actions and less guilt and stress from the impending leave date.

Choosing When and How You Listen

The Critical Voice is something we all deal with. The good news is you have a choice in how you think. Recognizing that the Critical Voice exists and is just one of many ways you think can be helpful in and of itself. And there is a myriad of other strategies to try—from sending it away to channeling your Wisdom Within to replace that voice. Sometimes it can be as simple as taking an action to move forward. It is amazing how much I have allowed my Critical Voice to hold me back from asking for a promotion or reaching out to network with someone, especially earlier in my career. You now have techniques to overcome that Critical Voice. Stop limiting yourself and empower the true you to come out.

Critical Voice Visualization Exercise

To allow you to concentrate on the exercise, you can find the recording at www.JenniferMarcou.com/resources.

Or consider recording yourself reading these instructions or having someone else read them to you. If you end up not visualizing anything, that is OK. Think of the exercise as a contemplation. Think about what your Critical Voice would think, say, or do. You may see lots of visuals or very few. All experiences are valid and valuable. Just note what you are seeing, feeling, or thinking at the end of the exercise.

Find a comfortable spot where you can sit. Make sure you have a pen and paper ready to take notes. This exercise should take about fifteen minutes.

Close your eyes. Take three deep breaths.

In through your nose—2—3—4. Out through your mouth—2—3—4.

In through your nose—2—3—4. Out through your mouth—2—3—4.

In through your nose—2—3—4. Out through your mouth—2—3—4.

Take one more breath in through your nose and breathe in until you feel you can't breathe in anymore, and take one more breath in through your nose, then breathe out through your mouth with a big sigh.

Now just return to normal breathing. Notice the rising and falling of your chest as you breathe normally.

Think of a time when you noticed your Critical Voice criticizing you, saying negative things.

What did your Critical Voice say?

What are other things your Critical Voice says?

What are the qualities of that voice? Is it mean, harsh, sassy, sarcastic, worried, risk averse, arrogant? Think of three words to describe that voice. What are the qualities of that voice?

When does that Critical Voice show up for you? What situations?

Does that voice have a gender? Is it male or female or neutral or neither?

What age do you think that voice is? Is it older or younger than you? Or the same age?

If your Critical Voice were a character from a book or movie or cartoon, what character would they be? What character would personify these characteristics? Or make up your own character. If you don't think of a character, think of a name you want to use to refer to this Critical Voice. What is this character's name?

What does your Critical Voice look like? What is it wearing?

What are your Critical Voice's motivations? What drives it?

Has your Critical Voice helped you in the past? And if so, how?

Now ask your Critical Voice the following questions. If you haven't thought about a character, that's OK. Just think about answering these questions in the way you think your Critical Voice would answer them.

Ask your Critical Voice how old it thinks you are.

If it thinks you are younger than you are, you can tell it that you are older now and you've got this.

Note what your Critical Voice does or says when you state that.

Can you ask your Critical Voice what it is afraid of?

Now, what role would you prefer your Critical Voice play? Encouraging you or being quiet or anything else?

Can you ask it to play that role? What would it have to stop or start doing to play that new role? And what does it say when you ask it to play that role?

Ask what its favorite leisurely activity is when it's not bugging you. Going to the beach, watching a movie, reading, fishing, hiking?

Think about something coming up in your life, where you expect your Critical Voice will show up. Imagine yourself before and/or during that event, asking your Critical Voice to:

- play a different role that you want it to play instead of speaking to you negatively. Imagine asking it to play a different role and noting what it does.
- do an activity that it enjoys doing—away from you. Imagine that it goes and does that activity while you continue on with whatever you're focused on.

Can you imagine that?

Now take one last breath on your count. In through your nose and, when you are ready, let it out through your mouth.

Now slowly open your eyes.

Debriefing Yourself

Please take a few minutes to write down what you saw, heard, and felt. Reflect on the responses you heard or contemplated from your Critical Voice. Which of the three strategies resonated with you the most?

- Was it just recognizing your Critical Voice exists and is just one of many ways to think of a situation that was so powerful?
- Or perhaps it was making the Critical Voice help instead of criticize you.
- Or perhaps it was sending the Critical Voice off, so you did not have to hear it.

Consider which strategy you might want to experiment with.

What If You Did Not See Anything in the Critical Voice Visualization?

Similar to the Wisdom Within exercise, if you did not visualize anything, that is completely valid, and there are some strategies to still benefit from this work:

- **Identify any details you did see.**

  Even the smallest detail or feeling can be helpful to understand your Critical Voice. Don't worry if you did not see or feel anything, or you just saw a big judging finger or some other visual came up for you. Think about what and how you felt when you saw that one visual.

- **Try the visualization another time.**

  You may want to try again when you are calmer or perhaps right after experiencing the Critical Voice. As with the Wisdom

Within visualization, if this exercise is overwhelmingly uncomfortable, consult a mental health professional for support.

- **Contemplate the questions and answer them from what you think your Critical Voice would say.**

  You can use this as simply a contemplation to understand what you are afraid of when that Critical Voice appears. Perhaps think about the source of that Critical Voice. Or just recognize that you have multiple perspectives in your head—that negative, critical view is just one of many.

What If You Pictured a Real Person as Your Critical Voice?

If you visualized a real person currently in your life right now—like a parent or boss or friend, try to take the characteristics of that person and create a new character so you are not thinking about that real person or referring to them by their real name. Separate your Critical Voice from the real people in your life who may have inspired or shaped your Critical Voice. You want to focus on what your Critical Voice says or does, not be thinking about what the real person would do or say.

ACTIONS TO CONSIDER

- Do the Critical Voice visualization exercise. Consider giving it a name and persona, being creative about sending it away, or reframing its role from critic to champion. What is your equivalent of "sending Miranda to a Paris fashion show"?
- Think about when your Critical Voice appears and what it says. What warning signals does it give?

continued

- Pick one of the 3R approaches for silencing or at least softening your Critical Voice (recognize, remove, rewire). Develop a small test using the LEAD framework.

Remember to download the Lead with Quiet Confidence workbook at www.JenniferMarcou.com/resources to help capture your insights on the Critical Voice visualization.

Part II Tool Review

Tools for Increasing Your Ability to Project Confidence

- Mentally reinforce the need to project confidence, not just competence.
- Practice the six ways to build and project confidence:
  - Calm your fears through exposure.
  - Find alternative methods for achieving a goal.
  - Learn new skills.
  - Prepare and practice.
  - Rewrite the negative stories in your head.
  - Have conviction.
- Use the components of your Inner Compass:
  - Use your Wisdom Within (revisit, channel, or emulate what your future best self would do).
  - Ask yourself whether this will matter in twenty years.
  - Become more mindful, breathing and connecting to your senses in the present moment.

  - Listen to your intuition.
  - Identify your purpose (both immediate and long-term).
  - Practice self-compassion (recognize emotions, recognize common humanity, encourage rather than self-criticize, take a small action).

- Use the two visualization exercises (Wisdom Within and Critical Voice).
- Learn to Recognize, Remove, and Rewire your Critical Voice.
  - Give your Critical Voice a name.
  - Find someplace you can send your Critical Voice (shopping, to Paris . . .), so they won't bother you!
  - Connect with your purpose instead of your worry.
- Change your reactions to negative events:
  - Identifying the gift
  - Reframing the situation
  - Showing gratitude
  - Taking one small step forward

PART III

BEHAVIORS:
Practical Guide to Being Successful as a Leader

If you are an introvert with career aspirations, you've probably heard all the criticisms I've faced in my career. My personal favorite was the feedback "Lead out in front." My introverted self and Critical Voice said internally, *You mean out in front where I am vulnerable and could get killed first?* Not helpful feedback.

There is no denying that effective leadership requires we introverts get out of our proverbial shell and put ourselves out there in ways that are neither natural nor comfortable for us. We have to get good at skills like speaking up, having executive presence, gaining visibility, influencing, and networking. We also know the day-to-day meetings and social events that are required of a leader can be very draining to introverts, and we need to carefully manage our energy so that we can recover and perform our best. These areas are important for success as a leader, particularly in large workplaces and communities where small-group or one-on-one communication may not be enough.

These areas have been personal challenges for me. How many times did I hear that I needed to not be so quiet or work on my executive presence? What is executive presence anyway? And then the dreaded "networking." Does that word send chills up your spine? And what does it take to influence others, which may be important to get what you want or make the changes in your work group or community?

As we discussed in an earlier chapter, competency and doing great work alone won't cut it if we want to become recognized as leaders. We can't assume others will see and recognize our efforts. We have to have visibility and be proactive about sharing our ideas, letting others know what we are doing, connecting with others. We have to "say it, send it, show up!"

This next section will provide tools and exercises to tackle the challenges of communicating in the workplace and help you harness the energy to keep you going. Specifically, we will find your unique leadership strengths and style as an introvert to influence others in your way. As always, it is a change in behavior, not a change in who you are.

8

Speaking Up

There's zero correlation between being
the best talker and having the best ideas.
—Susan Cain

A few years ago, I was on a conference call with three hundred other women in a training session where we were discussing how we can help clients overcome their fear of speaking up. I wanted to chime in about an experience I had advising my client to breathe before she speaks up, but I was nervous to say anything in front of so many people. I could hear my heartbeat in my ears, my cheeks getting warmer, my body getting agitated. My focus narrowed. I did not hear a word of what anyone was saying. I knew I had to say something, but I worried about what others would think, that what I would say was not important or smart.

When the call ended, I felt immediate relief that I had not spoken up. But soon after, I felt shame about not raising my hand. After all, I coach people to speak up all the time, so I am supposed to be able to do this. What was wrong with me?

This was all so ironic because this training was based on Tara Mohr's concept of Playing Big. We were all female coaches learning how to teach others to play bigger in their lives by making their voices heard. Although we were all supportive of each other because we are coaches, I was anxious and insecure about adding my thoughts, fearing embarrassment about sounding irrelevant or obvious. I didn't consider that my comments could help others.

It is intimidating to speak up, whether we are in a training session, a weekly staff meeting, or a senior leader discussion. If you have had a similar experience, you are not alone. In this chapter, I'll discuss ways to overcome these fears while staying true to your introvert self, starting with understanding why it's important to speak up.

Why It Is Important to Speak Up

In business school, I had a class on entrepreneurship. I have always been a strong, straight-A student. Part of the grade was based on class participation. Despite having done all of the homework and having done well on the tests and papers, I did not get an A in that class. Why? Because I did not say a word in class. I didn't think my contributions were valuable enough to share or worthwhile enough to overcome the energy it took for me to speak up. And I suffered the consequences. I broke my straight-A streak.

In the grand scheme of things, the grade itself was not important. But it was discouraging because at that point, I evaluated my success by the grade my teacher gave me. I wish I had learned earlier that grades don't matter; what matters is whether you feel you accomplished something. To make things worse, my friend (and future husband!) was in that class and a group project partner. He received the same grades on the group projects, but he participated more in class. He received an A, and to this day, he goads me about it.

There are all sorts of reasons why we don't speak up. I can speak from my own experience on that training call that I typically didn't want to speak up because I did not want people to judge me. I did not want to waste anyone's time with unhelpful or insignificant input. Does that sound familiar? A lot of my clients feel the same way because in general, introverts don't like the spotlight. We don't have all the answers. We think we are wrong. People may see that we are not really as smart as they thought we were. We don't want to bother others. We have not had enough time to think of something to say. Even if we have something to say, it may not be worth the energy it takes to say it in that moment. In addition, we have those critical voices that tell us we're not good enough or smart enough or deserving enough. Part of our brain—that Critical Voice discussed in Chapter 7—is fearful that horrible things could happen if we speak up. We may not get the next good project. We may get a bad review. We may end up without a job.

However, what didn't occur to me in that business school class or for a long time in the workplace was the impact of *not* speaking up. Your team, your customers, and your business are losing out by not hearing your ideas, thoughts, and questions. As introverts, we have different observations than others and think deeply about ideas. Our perceptions are valuable, and we can contribute to new ideas and ways to solve problems. And by not speaking up, *you* are missing out on having others react and build on your ideas, making them stronger. You are missing out on having more impact.

Over a third of my clients identify speaking up and being heard as things they want to work on in coaching. Before working with me, they think speaking up requires that they act like an extrovert, speaking constantly and over people, much to their distaste. Then they realize they can find their own way to speak up.

Speaking Up Without Mimicking an Extrovert: Kate's Story

Before every project meeting, Kate, a systems engineer at a health-care company, was nervous that she had to run the meeting and pretend to understand all the details of the project. She did not, and she was afraid someone would find out and fire her. Her role was to ensure clear system requirements by working collaboratively with customers, legal, risk management, and other employees and by delivering direction to the development team. In many meetings, she was not the expert but still had to make the call on what requirements were included. She had difficulty with impromptu speaking. She wanted to find her own authentic style of leadership without feeling like an impostor. Even though in her role she had to ask a lot of questions, she had been hesitant to ask those questions and push back on her partners.

Speaking up was important to Kate because she wanted her legacy to be having positively contributed to the advancement of health care that improves patients' lives. Getting the requirements right and aligning all the stakeholders was critical for her projects to succeed and to have that positive impact.

How did she get more comfortable speaking up?

To address Kate's fears, together we went through the Wisdom Within visualization exercise from Chapter 6. Kate visualized what her future self (whom she named Kathryn) would do in a stressful meeting situation. Kathryn had confidence and was calm in the face of stress. To emulate Kathryn, on the day of a stressful meeting, Kate would pick the outfit she felt most confident in. On the drive to work, she would think about how Kathryn would show up in the meeting—cool, calm, confident, and ready for engagement. Five minutes before the meeting, Kate would take a moment in the bathroom to pause and breathe. Then she would look at her notes of key questions she wanted to ask (and use as backups if she couldn't think on the spot). She would channel Kathryn, enabling her to be calm and confident in that moment.

Kate also learned how to connect to her purpose and facilitate the flow of information across the team. Through coaching, she got better at asking questions like, "What are we missing? When is the work going to be complete?" She came up with a personal strategy to compliment the partner first, then ask a question: "Great demo. I'd like to see more of your plans for this feature. Could you share this in the next meeting?" She moved from quiet and passive to becoming more assertive in her own style by asking questions.

She committed to speaking up in more meetings. And she had success. She was more comfortable asking questions that needed to be asked and pushing back on partners so the team could deliver the project.

When Kate caught herself asking internally, *Do I want to get into this right now?* or *What if my idea is wrong?*, she would access Kathryn to realize that for the good of the project, the team, and the customer, she needed to stop censoring herself.

In one particular meeting about continuous improvement of a project, Kate provided a dissenting viewpoint in her own way while still empathizing with the other side. "I think we can still achieve our launch date and conduct the customer research if we do the research and continue the product build concurrently instead of sequentially." The team had never executed that way before and they accepted how important getting the customer feedback was instead of skipping that step to hit the launch deadline. Not only did Kate speak up but in gathering the courage to do so, she opened her mind to creative ideas. Later, one team member said he appreciated that she shared her view because it gave the team a more well-rounded view of the problem and opportunities. This success enabled Kate to have the confidence to reach out to a former colleague and land a new, higher-level role in another company.

As we discussed in Chapter 3, repeated, small-dose exposure reduces fear of certain situations. That is exactly what Kate did as she tapped into her Wisdom Within and practiced speaking up. The more she did it, the easier it became, to the point that it became more natural. She did not need to transform into an extrovert.

> "Introverts are word economists in a society suffering from verbal diarrhea."
>
> —Michaela Chung of *The Irresistible Introvert*

Giving Yourself Permission to Speak: Jaden's Story

Jaden found she could speak up in recurring smaller meetings or when she had a lot of conviction, and it would bother her more if she did not say anything, such as standing up for a colleague. But she had challenges in larger meetings and with topics on which she did not have strong opinions. A content manager at a tech company responsible for creating and optimizing content across all marketing channels, she was ten years out of college but with a younger appearance and no formal background in marketing. Colleagues underestimated her experience and knowledge and did not acknowledge her in meetings. In her review, she got feedback from her boss that colleagues wanted to hear her opinions. With that reassurance, she did start to speak up more in larger groups. With a little more coaching, she realized that she could continue to speak up even without the "permission" or encouragement from her boss—she could simply remind herself of times she did speak up and the success and impact it had. For example, in one project, she wanted to recommend a new social media strategy. While it was new for her product, she had seen it work for another industry and felt it could work. It was risky, but she wanted to experiment with it. She decided to speak up early in the next meeting and recommended it to the group. After some debate, the team agreed to test it. As she shared excitedly with me, "I was part of the conversation!" She became her own permission-granter to speak up. She got promoted in her next review.

WHY SPEAKING UP IS MORE DIFFICULT FOR WOMEN

Historically, women have been raised to survive through likability. As Tara Mohr in *Playing Big* states, "For millennia, we [women] could ensure our survival by complying with what was approved of or desired by those with greater power. Being likable, or at least acceptable, to stronger, more powerful people was a survival strategy. This is part of why disapproval feels so unsafe to many women: For millennia, it was life threatening." Historically, women don't speak up because we want to be liked; we want to be agreeable.

Furthermore, research shows that women do indeed speak up less than men. Christopher Karpowitz and his colleagues' published research in the 2012 *American Political Science Review* found that women participate in meetings substantially less than men. Plus, "[t]he fewer women in the group, the lower their status, the less they may speak, and the lower their influence." Speaking up is a precursor to influence. Women already have a tough hurdle, and when you add on introversion, it becomes even more challenging as a female introvert to speak up.

Four Techniques for Speaking Up More Often and More Comfortably

Like Kate, connecting with the voice of your Wisdom Within can shift your thoughts to positive from negative and fear based. Your future self is likely calmer and more confident. Imagining how your future self would handle something allows you to channel them, think how they would think, act like they would act, and develop the courage to speak up. Here are four other tips for becoming comfortable with speaking up.

1. Prepare Ahead of Time

Remember from Chapter 2 that introverted brains work differently than extroverted brains. The introverted brain will take more time to process inputs from meetings to form a perspective. So that makes it difficult to have ideas on the spot the way many extroverts do. I always say that to get the best answer out of extroverts, ask them to answer a question on the spot. In contrast, to get the best answer out of introverts, ask them a question today and for an answer tomorrow. Introverts need time to process.

Given your brain chemistry, you are not going to think quicker. But you can leverage your strength of thoughtfulness by preparing for a meeting. A little bit of thinking beforehand can help you in the meeting. Here are some tips specifically:

- Review the agenda.
- Identify any issues to which you want to contribute ideas.
- Anticipate questions that may arise, and prepare standard responses to questions you don't know the answer to, like "Let me get back to you on that."
- Decide what you want your role to be—listener, contributor, facilitator, etc.

- Do research if you need to, but don't overly rely on this.
- Plan to send a follow-up email with your thoughts if they don't come during the meeting.

2. Apply the OARS Model When Asking Questions

Thinking fast enough to ask meaningful questions in the normal pace of conversation is a challenge for introverts. Having a model that gives you a framework for what questions to ask is really helpful for some people. I have applied the OARS model to help my coaching clients engage in business conversations and meetings where they may not want to participate or speak up, but they feel it is important to do so. Developed by William R. Miller and Stephen Rollnick, the OARS model was designed to help therapists ask questions and interact with their clients.

OARS is an acronym that stands for **o**pen-ended questions, **affir**mations, **r**eflective listening, and **s**ummarize (see Figure 8.1).

Figure 8.1: The OARS model for adding value with your voice

Here is a quick description of each of these steps:

- **Open-ended questions**: When talking with someone during a meeting, ask questions that can elicit a variety of answers: what, how, who, and why questions. If the answer to a question is yes or no or limited in some other way, then it is not an open-ended question. For example, instead of asking the closed question of "Is this our best option" (which requires a yes/no answer), ask the open-ended question, "What are the pros and cons of this option?" Open-ended questions engage others and get them talking to inform your perspective, enabling the team to explore a topic and come to conclusions.

- **Affirmations**: You can affirm other ideas and behaviors by responding with something you see. For example, "Sounds like you feel strongly and have lots of ideas about this." This integrates people into the conversation and shows that you are listening and reflecting. Affirmation can help share that unique perspective of what you're seeing in that meeting, in addition to moving the conversation along.
- **Reflective listening**: You can make comments like, "What I hear you saying . . . " or "A minute ago you mentioned X; how does that relate to Y?" This demonstrates leadership by steering the conversation.
- **Summarize**: This is my favorite. You can say things like, "Sounds like we're concluding X." You summarize what you are hearing to show that you are listening and participating. And you show that you drive results because you are getting to the conclusion. Similarly, the end of a meeting is a great time to state, "I think our next steps should be X, Y, and Z." Or you can even pose a question like, "When are we going to meet to discuss this?" Even though you may feel like you are not adding value because you're not bringing up new content, you are helping the group arrive at a conclusion by demonstrating your strong observational and reflection skills and drive for impact.

3. Ask "Anytime" Questions

Here is a series of what I like to call "anytime" questions that you could prepare ahead of time. These questions can be asked at nearly any point in any conversation and will help you and your team get more clarity. Sometimes asking the most basic question adds significant value. I will let you in on a little secret: These are very similar to questions I ask my coaching clients.

- What is our objective?
- What does success look like?
- How will we know we are done?
- What do we want to achieve in this meeting?
- Who else needs to be a part of this?
- Who else is impacted?
- What are we afraid to talk about?
- What are our ideas?
- What are we missing?
- What else?

PEOPLE DON'T REMEMBER WHAT YOU SAID; THEY REMEMBER THAT YOU CONTRIBUTED.

Pick one or two of these questions to ask in your next meeting. Sometimes even the most basic question like "What is our objective?" or "What are we trying to achieve in this meeting?" can be incredibly helpful for the group to align because everyone assumes that they know what this meeting is about, but many may not know or agree. By asking these "anytime" questions or using the OARS model, you are speaking up. People don't remember what you said; they remember that you contributed.

4. Follow Madeleine Albright's Advice

More advice comes from Madeleine Albright, the former US Secretary of State. She was a big proponent of women in leadership and developed tenets to help women who were quiet in meetings. I think her ideas are applicable to all introverts, no matter their gender.

- **Get heard early.** If you're nervous about speaking up, speak up early so you can get it over with quickly. More importantly, the ideas spoken early in a conversation are the ones that become the foundation to which other ideas are compared. You want your idea to be part of that foundation.
- **Don't bury your head in note-taking.** While it's comforting to bury our heads behind computers, in doing so our brains focus on the notes and what others are saying as opposed to formulating what we want to say. Stop taking so many notes and start contributing to the conversation.
- **Don't wait for the right moment; call on yourself.** There never will be a "right" moment. Introverts are very aware of when they interrupt and when others interrupt, so they are constantly waiting for the right moment to speak up. Extroverts, on the other hand, don't notice when they interrupt others, nor are they as bothered when they are interrupted because they are so focused on getting their message out. They're expecting others to interrupt them. So if you interrupt an extrovert, they probably won't even notice. Interrupt the interrupter.

DON'T WAIT TO BE CALLED ON—CALL ON YOURSELF.

- **Don't ask for permission and don't apologize.** Women tend to ask for permission—"Can I ask a question, please?" Men tend to just blurt out their questions. Similarly, women and introverts often apologize for taking time from others to speak up. Stop apologizing. Stop asking for permission. Just state what you want to state. Don't wait to be called on—call on yourself.

- **Stop others from interrupting you.** When someone interrupts you, you can put your hand up like a stop sign and say, "I'm not finished." This verbally and physically shows that you are still speaking. My husband loves to say, "Don't let the end of my sentence get in the way of the beginning of your sentence." Show that you recognize that the other person is interrupting you but that you still have something to say. The only way to change others' behaviors is by letting them know that what they're doing is not acceptable.

INTERRUPT THE INTERRUPTER.

- **Support others being interrupted.** Just as you need to stand up for yourself when you are interrupted, you also need to support others. When someone interrupts another person, you can say, "Hey, Jane was not done speaking. Let's let her finish." Chances are, as you stand up for others, others will stand up for you.

Reclaiming Your Ideas

For many years, if someone else spoke up and restated one of my ideas without giving me credit, I would just let it go. And then I'd steam and fume, annoyed that someone else got credit for my idea.

Eventually, I got bolder. I would send an email to the owner of the meeting and mention that I was happy that a couple of us came up with a particular idea. And I recruited allies, people who knew that, although I was quieter, I had good ideas, and they could speak up on my behalf.

It was usually my boss or perhaps a more senior colleague who would catch the person and say, "Hey, Jennifer just had that idea."

And then later in my career, I learned to say in-the-moment things like, "I just said that" or "I'm so glad you're building on my idea that I just said." Of course, it was hard, but I realized I just had to try. Now, I even quip, "I love that idea you got from me."

How to Be Heard

Sometimes we are not heard because we feel we are not allowed to speak. Once, I was in a meeting with four extroverts, including my boss. They were all talking over each other about a topic that they all agreed I was actually the expert on. But I could not get a word in edgewise. Frustrated, I finally slammed my hand down. For a split second, they all shut up and I had a moment to say what I wanted to say. This is not a strategy I use often. But there are ways you can use your body, like standing up, waving your hand, or making a noise, to get people's attention and create an opening for you to speak. Think creatively about what could work, even if it may be out of your comfort zone.

Here are four tips for getting heard:

1. Claim your idea by following up with an email. You may even want to sleep on it before writing to the meeting leader, as it will give your brain time to respond in the best way.
2. Reclaim your idea by stating in the meeting something like, "I like what you are building onto my idea."
3. Identify allies who can support you when you are interrupted or when someone states your idea without crediting you.
4. Make a physical move to get attention—slam hand down, stand up, wave your hand.

WHAT IF SOMETHING DOES NOT GO AS PLANNED?

What if that experiment doesn't work out the way you wanted? Maybe you spoke up, but no one listened. Think about what you learned in that situation. What are other ways to approach this? Maybe you need to speak louder. Maybe you need allies. Maybe you need to have an offline conversation with someone or send an email follow-up. Maybe you learned what not to do. Even when things don't work out as planned or hoped, there is always learning. In fact, as we learned earlier, sometimes there can be a gift when something doesn't go right. Perhaps you're getting stronger and more resilient. What if that lack of perfection in that experiment is just what you needed to learn to eventually perform at an even higher level?

Acknowledge Your Ideas Are Valuable

During the training program I described at the beginning of this chapter, I ended up having twenty-four conference calls with those three hundred women. And I never got up the guts to go off mute and speak, which was bad for me and bad for the rest of the participants, as I am sure someone would have found value in my comments. But a year later, I took a training course with the same teacher and in the same large format. I gave myself a goal to speak up at some point. The program was shorter, so I decided to speak up sooner rather than later. (Thank you, Madeleine Albright!)

In one of the earlier sessions, we were talking about giving ourselves empathy. I wanted to share a personal challenge I was having in accepting my mother's dementia. I was very vulnerable and emotional. I wrote down what I wanted to say on a sticky note, so I would not forget in the anxiety of the moment. Determined to overcome my fear, I raised my hand. My heart was racing. And when called on, I shared the story of when my mom was diagnosed with dementia, and I was so angry that I had to do her taxes, close down her business, and move her. I shared other details of what I'd lost, such as realizing I would never again have her tell me she was proud of me and how I'd needed to learn to apply empathy to myself.

The response I got from the other participants on the call was overwhelming. I had an impact. I received many positive comments in the chat from others experiencing something similar. One woman said that she, too, had been angry about her mom's dementia, but my story helped her realize that she had to give herself empathy instead of beating herself up. That challenge to myself to speak up paid off. It helped me and it helped others. Use your voice to add value. Your ideas have impact. Just say it!

ACTIONS TO CONSIDER

- Reflect on times you wanted to contribute to a discussion but didn't. What held you back? What would it have taken in those situations to give you the confidence to speak up?
- Review the strategies for speaking up more comfortably. Pick one and do a test of how well that strategy works for you.
- Before any meeting or conversation, think about your purpose in participating. What would be lost if you didn't speak up?
- Before an important meeting, channel your Wisdom Within or Madeleine Albright. How would those people handle the situation you're facing?

Remember you have access to the *Lead with Quiet Confidence Workbook* at www.JenniferMarcou.com/resources to help you to capture your thoughts and things you want to experiment with.

9

Executive Presence

Our deepest fear is not that we are inadequate.
Our deepest fear is that we are powerful beyond measure.
It is our light, not our darkness, that most frightens us.
We ask ourselves, "Who am I to be brilliant, gorgeous,
talented, fabulous?" Actually, who are you not to be?
—Marianne Williamson

Have you received feedback to improve your executive presence? Did you understand what was being asked of you? Were you told how others wanted you to show up? I have experienced this many times in my life, and I never got a satisfactory answer regarding what I needed to do differently.

"Executive presence" is such an ambiguous term. It seems to fall into the "I can't define it, but I know it when I see it" category. According to research by Tracom Group, 51 percent of HR practitioners believe executive presence is difficult to define. At the same time, 81 percent of them believe it is easy to spot. Executive presence is an intangible quality.

According to *Forbes* magazine, executive presence is **your ability to inspire confidence in three groups**:

1. Inspiring confidence **in your subordinates** that you're the leader they want to follow
2. Inspiring confidence **among peers** that you're capable and reliable
3. Most importantly, inspiring confidence **among senior leaders** that you have the potential for great achievements

As you can see, executive presence creates confidence from above, below, and beside you. We should cultivate our executive presence because it's a core quality of many senior leaders. They are confident, trustworthy, and assertive; have expertise and strong interpersonal skills; and deliver results. The majority of companies surveyed by Tracom are looking for executive presence in their senior leaders. Executive presence was a required competency for high-potential employees. If you want to move up in your organization, you will need to find your executive presence. Luckily, while it's elusive to define, it can be taught—even to introverts. I eventually codified what it means to me and how I can practice it and have now successfully taught clients to do the same. In this chapter, I'll share what I've learned about executive presence.

Start Off as You Mean to Continue: Ginny's Story

It's happening again! Ginny was saying to herself. *Everyone is looking at me, and I can't say anything coherently. Come on, brain. Say something smart!*

As an engineering manager at a biotech firm, Ginny had to present to leadership her team's plans for a new product. Before we started working together, she would be so nervous that she could not even start to speak. She would stumble over her words. And the more she stuttered, the worse she would feel. However, once she got over that initial stumbling, she was OK. It was the initial few sentences that tripped her up and ruined her chances of appearing a confident leader. Ginny wanted to work on presenting to senior leaders and larger audiences, particularly working on starting off strong.

Together, we channeled her Wisdom Within, herself in twenty years. She said her Wisdom Within was "the coolest person she knows."

Ginny identified situations where she was *not* nervous to speak and naturally acted like her Wisdom Within, which were usually when talking with or presenting to a senior leader she knew well. She realized that when she focused on telling the truth and having a conversation instead of worrying whether she was going to say the wrong thing or what people were thinking about her, she spoke successfully.

She took that insight and confidence to new situations, such as when she was asked to present at a large conference in Florida. She first imagined how her Wisdom Within would present: confident, casual, and friendly. She treated her presentation like a conversation and practiced her first few sentences. And once she got started, she felt she did great. Strangers came up afterward and told her how engaging she was on stage. Her boss was proud and noted how confident she appeared to be.

Despite her preparation, Ginny was surprised the presentation went so well and asked herself, *Who was that person?* She then realized that confident person was her. That confidence was in her the whole time; it just took some channeling her Wisdom Within for it to come out. Let's talk about how we can find that executive presence within you.

What Does Executive Presence Look Like in a Quiet Leader?

Think of a quiet leader who you think has executive presence. Use your introverted strengths of observation and reflection. Maybe it's her calm demeanor or his pausing to let others speak. Observe what that leader does and says. Reflect on how that leader makes you feel when you are in their presence. Are they fully present, making good eye contact, not multitasking? Do they make you feel heard by nodding or asking questions? Identify specifically what that person does or says that makes you feel that way. Identify ideas you want to try in building your own executive presence.

When I think of a quiet leader with executive presence, I think of Ken Chenault, former chairman and CEO of American Express. I don't know if he is actually an introvert, but he exhibits behaviors that introverts should emulate. When I was the vice president of online marketing for American Express, launching our first internal corporate intranet, I had the honor of presenting to him every two weeks for several months. While he had a very busy schedule, he was always on time for our meetings. He always asked what the goal of the meeting was. He'd always listen for the first five minutes, and if we were not getting to the part he was interested in, he would calmly ask a question or redirect the conversation to the issue that was top of mind for him, such as potential savings from reengineering or the change management required to get employees to use the new site. He was calm and approachable but not afraid to challenge you in a respectful way.

Observing him in larger town halls, he was the essence of executive presence: confident, a skilled and unflappable communicator. He brought the entire company together for a town hall in Madison Square Garden after September 11, 2001, when the World Trade Centers collapsed across the street from American Express headquarters, forcing us to relocate for several months. He showed empathy and poise, was honest and transparent about what he knew and did not know, and gave us hope that despite the global shutdown of travel, we as a travel and financial services company would survive. He gave us confidence that he could lead us through this challenging emotional and economic time. He was not getting us riled up. He stated facts of how we were going to work in a collection of offices around New York City. He connected with emotions of fear for our safety, fear for the health of our company and industry, and fear that things would never be the same.

There were tears in my eyes and those of many others in the audience. He also provided hope, painting a vision that we would be stronger from this challenge. He did not know all the answers to what the future would hold, but you believed him that things were going to be all right. After that remarkable town hall, I evolved from wondering if I would be laid off due to the economic downturn and state of the travel industry to being cautiously optimistic and connected and in community with my fellow employees.

I am sure Ken Chenault has had many memorable speeches in his career, but as an employee, I felt that was the most impactful one I'd experienced. It is not often that a leader can touch each soul in the audience and lead confidently in the face of uncertainty. I as a leader and we as a company had confidence that he was going to lead us out of the fear and ambiguity of the economy and the future of our company. That is the kind of leader that I want to be: calm, confident, transparent, empathetic, and action oriented. And it starts with executive presence.

3Cs of Executive Presence

When I was mid-level in my career, I got feedback like, "Your presentation was fine, but you did not present like an executive." When I asked how an executive would present, I was told, "Well, differently." That was not helpful.

Competence is the sole area that introverts tend to focus on. We use our strong, thoughtful brains to explore and learn more in our subject-matter expertise. When a presentation is coming up, we tend to focus on the content of the presentation, which is our area of expertise. But as we learned in Chapter 4, confidence is more important than competence. And yes, as I grew in my career, my confidence grew, yet I still did not know what executive presence was, nor could anyone define it. So I decided to actively observe leaders who I thought were effective, like Ken Chenault; Al Kelly, president of American Express and then chairman and CEO of Visa; and Satya Nadella, chairman and CEO of Microsoft. And I realized there was a third *C* I needed to add to *confidence* and *competence*: *communication* (resulting in the 3Cs as shown in Figure 9.1). To be an introvert with executive presence, we have to practice all three of these Cs.

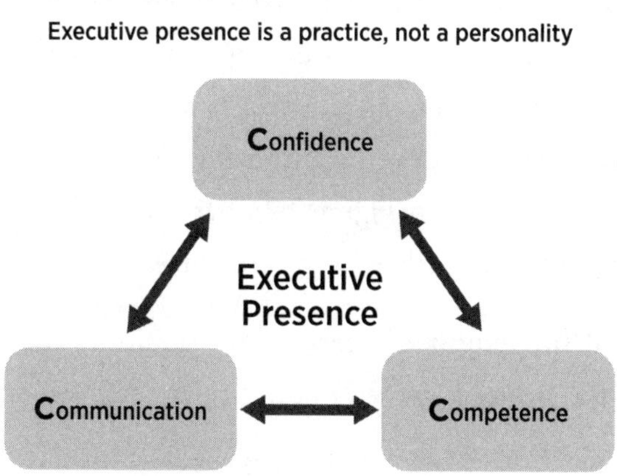

Figure 9.1: 3Cs of executive presence

Confidence

As we learned in Chapter 4, confidence is core to leading with your authentic self. It also can be learned through taking action and practicing.

Practice

Having executive presence is a skill that can be acquired through practice; "charismatic" people are not the only ones who have it. Executive presence is a practice, not a personality. You can practice showing up every day in your meetings with more confidence, more eye contact, a smile, maybe even some chitchatting (but pick a topic you are interested in). Make sure you have built up some energy to exude some of that energy in the meeting. Remember, executive presence is inspiring confidence in those around you just in how you show up, whether you are presenting or not.

EXECUTIVE PRESENCE IS A PRACTICE, NOT A PERSONALITY.

When you do present, practicing your presentation or practicing sharing your perspective is a good way to build confidence. Introverts in general are good at preparing. I talked about practicing in Chapter 4, but here I want to focus on specific steps you can take that will contribute to your executive presence. For me, whenever I had to present, I would practice over and over again in the mirror beforehand. I also practiced for three scenarios (Figure 9.2) that would allow me to accommodate for potential (and likely) time crunches.

- **Planned/full length**—Hitting all the points on the pages and telling the stories I wanted to use to bring my points home.
- **Quick version**—One minute per page, so I hit each key point on every page in a concise way.

Figure 9.2: Three scenarios of presentations to practice

- **Elevator speech**—Share all the insights and asks in thirty to sixty seconds (as long as it takes to go up an elevator). I have to do it by memory without slides. I have to be pointed in my statements. For example, "We are over budget by $10K this year due to increased cost of goods. We plan to change suppliers and that will save $50K next year. But until we fully transition, we need an extra $10K budget for this year." (The full presentation would have gone into all the details and options we looked at.)

Thinking through these scenarios reduced my level of stress and worry and allowed me to project calmness during the presentation.

The trick, of course, is figuring out how much practice is just right. You don't want to get to a point where your speech seems canned or overly prepared. You still want energy in your voice. I know just the right amount of preparation that helps soothe my nerves and makes me feel more confident yet still leaves enough nerves to keep me excited.

You will need to find the right amount of practice for you and determine what you need to practice so you can feel confident. For me, it's the time-crunch scenarios, but you may have other factors you need to address.

Reflect on Your Past Success

Reflect on times when you felt confident in the past or when you overcame your nerves and became confident. Maybe it was asking for a promotion for someone on your team or asking your child's teacher for extra help in a subject they were struggling in. Build on your past success by remembering how you felt. Convicted? Clear? Optimistic? How did your body feel? Calm? Energized? Relaxed?

One time, I was presenting to a room of one hundred coworkers. I had presented to that size audience before, but they had been complete strangers and I had no problems. But for some reason, presenting to that audience of colleagues made me more nervous, and my hands started shaking. So I pretended the audience members were all strangers I would never see again. It gave me confidence to stay up on stage without my hands shaking.

Prepare Physically and Mentally

Body language can give you confidence or betray a lack of confidence. Amy Cuddy, social psychologist and best-selling author, has done a lot of research about how body position impacts you internally. Specifically, she discovered that "holding high-power poses for just two minutes led to hormonal changes, increasing testosterone by about 20 percent and decreasing cortisol by about 25 percent. In other words, participants had increased feelings of dominance and decreased feelings of stress." Positioning our body in power stances can help ready your body and hormones to perform at the highest level.

Similarly, communications expert Denise Dudley found that pretending to put your hands in your front pants pockets sets your shoulders in the right position for an upright posture. For those of us with poor posture, it may feel like your shoulders are too far back, but this is actually a natural upright posture.

Think about adopting an expansive posture—such as an open chest, with hands on hips and chin slightly lifted—for just two minutes to increase your confidence levels and project power, competence, and charisma. Try it before a meeting. Go somewhere you can't be observed (your office, a bathroom, an unused hallway) and stand with your hands on your hips (or pretend to put them in front pockets) and your legs apart like a superhero.

As part of physical and mental preparation, manage your body's response to stress through mindfulness or slow deep breaths before, during, or after a meeting or presentation. Doing so will help you feel more calm, centered, and confident. Or take a walk before to calm your nerves.

Lastly, consider this: Not all physical reactions are negative. For instance, increased heart rate and sweaty palms are ways to prepare you for performance even though we view them as negative signs of nervousness or lack of confidence. According to Lisa Feldman Barrett in her research titled "Theory of Constructed Emotion," we construct and perceive emotion from the bodily sensations our brain receives, such as "sweaty palms mean nervousness," which the brain interprets as lack of confidence. But her research shows that reframing your body's response as *excitement* rather than *anxiousness* can increase performance.

Combining this advice can help you create a ritual before you present, such as finding a quiet space and deep breathing for five minutes or doing a power pose in the bathroom mirror or talking to yourself in third person, like "Jennifer, you've got this. Your heart is racing to prepare you to perform. You have butterflies in your stomach as you are excited to share your expertise. It's going to go great." Find the techniques that work for you.

These techniques work not just for presentations but in other work situations and everyday life. Interviewing for a new job, going into meetings that could be contentious, introducing yourself to a stranger, leading a team meeting, or sharing a perspective in a training class are all examples where you can use these strategies of appearing and being more confident to have greater impact.

Wear What Makes You Feel Confident

Your appearance matters: It impacts people's perceptions of you and your confidence and reflects your own feelings about yourself. With the change in workplace styles to more casual attire, it can be hard to identify what to wear.

There is compelling evidence that says wear what you feel best in. Researchers at Northwestern identified the concept of "enclothed cognition," which describes the influence that clothes can have from both a symbolic standpoint and the physical experience of wearing them. Specifically, people performed better on an accuracy test when they wore a lab coat than a white "painter's coat" (which was exactly the same as the lab coat) versus no additional coat.

Other studies showed that men who wore a suit in negotiations increased the likelihood of more profitable deals and those who dressed down had lower testosterone levels. What the subjects wore impacted their cognitive performance and their biological reactions, which is very compelling evidence to wear clothes that make you feel confident. I discovered that wearing a jacket to presentations or important meetings makes me feel more powerful and in charge. I always wear comfortable clothing, so I can focus on the presentation rather than clothes that are itchy or too tight.

CHANNELING YOUR WISDOM WITHIN

As we've discussed in a previous chapter, your Wisdom Within is a great source of confidence. How would yours show up to a meeting? What adjectives would you use to describe them? *Confident* is probably one of the words you would use. What would your Wisdom Within do to prepare for the presentation? What would they do if something did not go as planned? What would they wear?

Communication

The second *C* of executive presence is communication, which is how you exchange information, written or verbal. Even if you have the greatest idea, nothing will happen unless you effectively communicate it.

A large part of communication is speaking up in the first place, as we discussed in the last chapter. But there are ways to frame your communication that can contribute to your executive presence. Here are suggestions that can help introverts specifically.

Be Clear in Your Own Mind About Your Ideas or Vision

Remember, the introverted brain needs time to think before the meeting, so read agendas and come prepared with ideas, perspectives, and questions. Think in advance about what points you want to make in a meeting, even if you are not presenting. If you are a presenter, prepare the main points of your presentations as discussed in the first *C* (confidence) section. The clearer you are in your mind, the more likely you are to contribute in meaningful ways during a conversation or meeting.

Tell Stories

As an introvert, I spent much of my life not wanting to share feelings or personal details. But then I realized that when I did share something from my life, I was perceived as more approachable and friendlier. And as Brené Brown says, you have to be vulnerable to be brave. As Maya Angelou says, "People will forget what you said, people will forget what you did, but people will never forget how you made them feel." Good stories make you feel something.

When preparing for a meeting or presentation, find a personal story or customer story or perhaps something in the news that connects with your main point, so you can connect more easily with your audience. That connection will increase their trust in you and inspire confidence that you are a leader to follow.

I have followed this advice and started sharing more. For example, in a large town hall at Microsoft, I shared that I grew up loving the '80s band the Thompson Twins. I mentioned their hit "Hold Me Now" as a way to show that we had to "hold" our customers and show them more empathy. I even played the song at the end. My colleagues loved it, and the team said it was memorable and made the point. People reported that they felt they knew me better through this method rather than the all-business presentations I had previously done. I was being authentically me.

Rest assured, you don't have to reveal anything you don't want to. But find a story that supports your point. In fact, I'll bet you won't remember all the points I made in this book but will likely remember one or more stories. Tell stories to make your points stick.

Improve Your Presentation Skills

Practice the basics of strong communication. Make eye contact. Find friendly faces in the crowd and bounce your eyes among them. Slow down and pause. As introverts, we may want to use as little space and time as possible, so we speak quickly. But slowing down can enable your audience to hear your points, and pausing can help them sink in. A real power play in a presentation is to pause before you start. People will perk up and listen closely as they wait for you to start.

As I mentioned in Chapter 4, I was not a natural presenter and felt uncomfortable being the center of attention. I never raised my hand to present, so I did not get practice. In business school, I realized I needed to learn to be a good presenter. Joining Toastmasters enabled me to learn and practice presentation skills. Now I don't mind public speaking. Public speaking is often easier for introverts than cocktail chitchat because we can practice and it is more controllable. Net-net, presentation skills can be learned, practiced, and refined.

Communicate at the Right Altitude

To communicate at the right level, you need to know what is important to the audience, what they need to know, and at what level. Don't think that your love of details is what everyone else wants to hear. For a long time, I'd tend to present to senior leaders all the details that I would want to know. That's because we introverts love to think deeply and may mistakenly believe that others want to go as deep as we do. But I learned over time that senior leaders in general do not want to know the details; rather, they want to know the big ideas and issues. So I learned to focus on the executive summary, as that was usually the only page in a deck I would be able to get to when presenting to a very senior leader.

This is true of all conversations you have with senior leaders, no matter the context. If they ask you a question, get to core issue, challenge, or request quickly. Don't go deep into the details or start from the beginning, unless they ask you to. We will learn more about effectively communicating to your audience in the next chapter.

Competence

The third *C* of executive presence is competence. As I mentioned before, this is an area that introverts usually thrive in. We love to go deep into a topic; we love researching, learning, and reading. So this is less of a focus for most of my introverted coaching clients. Still, here are some tips for elevating your competence.

Know Your Content

It is critical to know your content. Anticipate questions the audience may have and prepare answers in advance. Also, prepare a statement to make if you don't know the answer during the presentation or meeting. For example, you can reply, "Great question. Let me get back to you on that."

Contribute in Other Ways If You Don't Know the Content

If you are presenting on behalf of someone else, learn the key points before presenting a topic. You will likely not have time to become an expert, but take the time to anticipate the key questions your audience may have and prepare responses beforehand. If someone asks you a question you don't know, state your prepared response, like "I don't know the specifics. I can get back to you." And make sure you do. Knowing the introverted mind, you will give your best response with some time to process.

If you are simply participating rather than presenting in a meeting on content you are not an expert on, don't be afraid to contribute in other ways by providing your perspective or asking questions. Again, the OARS model from Chapter 8 on speaking up can give you a framework to ask questions, make affirmations, use reflective listening, and summarize.

Executive Presence and Introversion Are Not Opposites

Late in my career, as a general manager of marketing at Microsoft, I was in a leadership training, which required student participation, something I dislike. But I was passionate about the material, so I did speak up and share. At the end of the training, a leader and participant whom I had never met complimented me, saying I had "quiet gravitas." He added that while I had not said much, when I did speak up, it had impact. That comment proved to me that 1) I should continue to speak up because I can add value, and 2) I can have impact in my own quiet way. I realized I needed to "show up!"

You can improve your executive presence. It is not an esoteric trait you are born with or not. With practice, you can get more confident, become a better communicator, and become more competent. All of these traits will lead you to having more executive presence, so you can shine like the millions of introverted leaders in the world—but in your own way.

You have to trust yourself that you have got this. You, too, can be quiet and introverted and still project executive presence. It just takes practice.

ACTIONS TO CONSIDER

- Reflect on how you would define executive presence. How can you find out which of those traits other people perceive in you and which they don't?
- Consider an event or interaction you have coming up in the next week or two where executive presence would be helpful to you. Try experimenting with one thing that will help you project executive presence in that situation. As you improve in that area, you can go back to the list

continued

of other things you want to work on but do them one at a time. You are more likely to be successful in changing behavior if you try one thing at a time and give yourself Kind goals or experiments.

As always, refer to the *Lead with Quiet Confidence Workbook* at www.JenniferMarcou.com/resources for more reflection questions and actions you can take to practice.

10

Visibility and Influence

Lighthouses don't go running all over an island looking
for boats to save; they just stand there shining.
—Anne Lamott

I was crying in the forest outside my office building at Microsoft, where I had been working for six years. Thankfully, no one was there. I'd just found out that I did not get the general manager job, a role I'd been filling as the interim leader. No question I had the subject-matter expertise in digital marketing and had been building my experience leading a larger team of forty. I had the respect of the team, my colleagues. But I did not get the job. Why?

The person who was selected certainly had more leadership experience but had no specific experience in digital marketing, which was the team's focus. I was resentful because, in my introvert way, I had assumed that knowing the content and having strong leadership skills would be enough for me to get the job. I thought it would be enough to bring the subject-matter expertise to secure the job for me. But it was not. The new leader had executive sponsorship from a very senior leader who was grooming her. Unlike me, she had worked in multiple parts of the organization and was well known. Later, I realized there was also some luck involved. She was ready to move on from her previous role, the general manager role was open, and they knew that I would stay and work hard under her. Good timing for her. Bad timing for me.

The decision-maker explained the choice was not about my leadership competency or knowledge but rather that the other candidate had more leadership experience. I grew to love and respect this new leader and learned a lot working with her, especially about extroverted styles. I saw the power in her staying visible to leaders to make sure our team got the resources we needed. I saw the influence she gained by making connections across the organization, allowing her to leverage resources or to identify new ways to structure our planning or to scout talent. She had qualities that I wanted to grow in myself: visibility and influence.

VISIBILITY IS AS MUCH A TOOL FOR CAREER GROWTH AS EXPERTISE AND HARD WORK.

Now I look at that result as a powerful learning experience. The lesson was a hard but impactful one: Visibility is as much a tool for career growth as expertise and hard work. It requires intention, strategy, and, often, stepping outside an introvert's comfort zone. I realized my lack of visibility outside my direct organization had cost me not only a job that I was well suited for but would have cost my team the resources and information we needed to be successful had I gotten the job instead of the woman who did.

How many times have you wanted to be more visible or received feedback that you should be? Have you been passed over for promotions and recognition because you were not comfortable speaking about yourself and your accomplishments or because you weren't perceived as a person of influence?

I don't know about you, but visibility doesn't come naturally to me. It feels dreadful to toot my own horn. And, not surprisingly for an introvert, I mistakenly thought that influence would come from competency. Despite the challenges, I learned how to achieve visibility and influence in ways that introverts can be comfortable with, and I'll share those lessons with you in this chapter.

Improving Visibility

Let me tell you the rest of my "passed over for general manager" story. After working for my boss for a year, with her observing my strengths and areas for development, I asked her about a promotion to the next level in marketing. It would be a big jump from senior director to general manager. It required approval of the CMO (chief marketing officer) and some head-nodding from his corporate vice presidents. My boss kept telling me to get out there and connect with people across the company, particularly other senior leaders in marketing, so they would get to know me. She was happy to facilitate. But I hated reaching out to people to share best practices. I felt concerned they would not agree to meet with me or would not want my best practices. But I did take her up on her offer to facilitate a few connections. I did enjoy learning about other areas. So, I did my best.

Specifically, I got involved in a newly formed Women's Leadership Initiative across all of marketing. I'd been passionate about helping female leaders ever since attending a women's high school, and I had been involved in the women's group previously at American Express. I was always inspired by my mother, who broke barriers in leadership as a female account executive in advertising and then became an entrepreneur starting her own advertising business, then a documentary filmmaker.

I had been leading a women's group for hundreds of employees in my business unit, sharing all our learnings and best practices freely with the new corporate vice president (CVP). We worked closely together to create this new, broader group for thousands of marketing professionals. The CVP was appreciative of my contributions and leadership. She said we had the best-organized and most-impactful women's leadership groups across all of the marketing groups. The CVP modeled her program after ours, incorporating mentoring and internal speakers.

The CVP was also on the marketing leadership team, which was the group that made recommendations and decisions on promotions to the general manager level, my next level. Connecting with the CVP was comfortable, even though I did not know her at all. I was in my element and did great work with her because of this passion for supporting women and their careers.

Lo and behold, a few months later, not even in the normal promotion cycle, I was promoted to general manager. I was in shock. I was not expecting it. I had stopped asking for it. My boss said the CMO and executive team were supportive of my promotion not only because of the work I did in my regular day job of digital marketing but also because of my leadership in the Women's Leadership Initiative.

I attribute this career advancement directly to growing my visibility with a broader network of people in the organization. Importantly, I did not do it in an artificial way. Rather, I used my passion to find an area where I could naturally contribute. I had no problem sharing the results of the work we did on the Women's Leadership Initiative with senior leaders, as it was not about tooting my horn; it was about something bigger: developing female leaders, a purpose I believed in.

SILENCE YOUR CRITICAL VOICE

I used to fear sending update emails to senior leaders several levels above me. I did not want the spotlight on me, or I did not want to bother them or be vulnerable in case I said something wrong. I said to myself, *They won't know who I am. I won't say the right thing. My boss will get mad. I am not following the right hierarchical protocol. I will look stupid or inappropriate or arrogant.*

As I learned, those fears were usually unfounded. Leaders rarely spend much time evaluating the quality of an email. I decided to view sending status emails as providing value to inform decisions or help senior leaders connect the dots between projects. I was helping the leader rather than promoting myself.

Fear of performance, fear of perceptions, or fear of something new are all strong emotions. Use the strategies from Chapter 7 to minimize or refocus those fears. It just takes courage and using one or two of those strategies. Remind yourself to just "send it!"

Developing a Visibility Plan

A plan to increase your visibility should address the following four areas:

1. **Why** you want to be more visible
2. **What** you want to be visible for
3. **Who** you want to be visible to
4. **Tactics** you'll use to become more visible

Let's discuss each of these areas.

1. *Why* Do You Want to Be More Visible?

Think strategically about why you want visibility instead of just thinking of it as something you "should" do. Perhaps you want to get selected for special or stretch projects, rewards, or maybe even promotions.

2. *What* Do You Want to Be Visible For?

There is good visibility and bad visibility. Bad visibility is, for example, when your error is front and center or you are working on a failing project that people associate with you. Good visibility is ensuring your unique strengths and accomplishments are recognized and valued within your organization. Think about what you want to be known for.

3. *Who* Do You Want to Be More Visible To?

Be very conscious about whom you want to be visible to based on why you want to be visible. Is it just your boss? Is it your boss's boss? The head of the department? Other colleagues? Your team? Someone in another department? If your goal is to get promoted, you'll want to be visible to your boss and likely your skip level, and perhaps the colleagues of your boss who may be in the room when promotions are discussed.

4. What *Tactics* Will You Use to Become More Visible?

In my last couple of jobs at Microsoft, I wanted to be known for being customer focused and being a great leader of people. In regular business meetings, I made sure to ask questions like, "What is the impact to the customer?" I earned a reputation for being customer focused.

I also made sure that I stepped up for projects that would showcase those two areas of focus. In addition to leading the women's group, I asked questions in staff meetings with other leaders about how we could better develop and train our employees. I was always well prepared for discussions with other leaders about aligning on employees' ratings for year-end reviews—not only to comment on my team but to comment on others to support their development. I took time to get to know others in the organization, and I spent a lot of time mentoring.

I took planned actions to use my strengths and to showcase them but not in a showy way. I showcased them by doing what I loved and what I felt was important to the business and my job.

Humility and not being in the spotlight can be important to introverts, so self-promotion can feel wrong. Alan Morinis, author of *Everyday Holiness*, has a famous saying: "No more than my space, no less than my place." Introverts are good at not taking up too much space, but make sure you are taking your place in the meeting, in the business, in the world. It does not need to be self-promotion.

As another example, if your goal is to be asked to take on special projects, build relationships by inviting people for coffee or lunch if you are working with people you have not worked with before. Ask for a thirty-minute one-on-one with leaders in other areas that you are interested in. Think of it as building a relationship versus trying to be visible. It won't happen unless they know about you or unless you specifically ask. Your leader and colleagues can help provide opportunities to be more visible.

I've summarized other common tactics for visibility in Table 10.1.

"Anytime" Strategies for Increasing Visibility
Speak up in meetings.
Talk to the target person before or after meetings.
Send an email to the target person with ideas, feedback, or follow-up.
For Online Meetings
Have your camera on and look engaged in the conversation.
Do not multitask during the call.
Use the chat function to add input or ask questions.
Raise your hand to speak.
Send IMs/chats, if appropriate, to key people (e.g., your boss or agenda owner) if you have ideas or input but are having trouble getting a word in edgewise.
Send an email with ideas that may come up after the meeting or if you were not able to speak.
For Broader Visibility of You or Your Team's Work
Highlight your accomplishments in your weekly/biweekly update with your boss.
Send out a newsletter highlighting what would be helpful for others to know or learn from.
Hold an info-share session like a lunch-and-learn, in the spirit of helping others learn (not tooting your own horn).
Volunteer to present at a team or company event.
Volunteer for a special task force or employee resource group that is more visible.
Use your resources and contacts: • Ask your boss for opportunities to be more visible—presentations or special projects or projects with teams with which you want to develop relationships. • Ask your boss for connections/introductions to people you want to be more visible to. • Ask colleagues who seem to be more visible how they became so.

Table 10.1: Example strategies for increasing visibility

VISIBILITY FOR WOMEN

Female introverts need to work even harder at getting visibility because the strategies that work for men don't always work for women. Research by Catalyst studying three thousand high-potential MBA graduates, published in their report titled "The Myth of the Ideal Worker: Does Doing All the Right Things Really Get Women Ahead?," found that the single most important thing women can do for their career advancement is **communicate their achievements to their bosses**. Furthermore, Catalyst identified that "doing all the 'right things' such as being proactive, requesting high profile assignments, and asking for promotions and raises, did not significantly help women advance their careers." The study states, "Women must adopt strategies different from their male colleagues to advance their careers. When women were proactive in making their achievements known, they advanced further, increased their compensation, and were more satisfied with their careers. . . . In other words, how you accomplish what you do and how you publicize those accomplishments appear to be equally important." So share your achievements—send that email to your boss on your accomplishments this week.

From Quiet Worker to Visible Problem-Solver: Kai's Story

Kai, a technical product manager, started a new job at a medium-size online payment company. He wanted to build his visibility at the company, especially with the leadership team. In his new company, no one knew his reputation, and he kept quiet about his work.

In our coaching sessions, he identified the following key components of his plan:

- Why he wanted to be known: to assimilate into the company, build relationships quickly to better collaborate to get his projects completed, and build a career path for his next role within the company
- What he wanted to be known for: analytical, customer focused, and good problem-solver
- Who he wanted to be known by: his boss, the head of Product, the head of Engineering, and the CEO. He also wanted to have a good relationship with marketing colleagues.
- Tactics: He made a plan to meet formally with each party monthly, first just to get to know each other, then talking about key business issues as well as keeping them informed of his progress. He would send out monthly emails to the broader audience of the progress he was making.

At first, Kai was highly uncomfortable, but he got positive feedback from that first email, which others found helpful. Two months later, a colleague, prompted by the update on his project email, came to him to problem-solve an area he was working on. If it had not been for Kai's email, that collaboration would likely never have happened. Kai became known as a great problem-solver. Kai continued to let his boss know not only about his accomplishments in their weekly update but also about the relationships he was building across the company. His boss helped him realize that operations was a key group to build relationships with. He received a promotion within his first year. And in that short time, Kai was much better known at his new company than he was after ten years at his last company. Kai was able to grow visibility in a way that was not too far out of his comfort zone and was natural and productive.

Visibility does not need to be an evil, uncomfortable thing for introverts. It can be planful, an introvert strength, to ensure others are seeing your accomplishments and leadership. You can be in control of it. Just don't leave it to chance.

Visibility isn't about seeking the spotlight—it's about letting your work be seen. You just have to "say it, send it, show up." Let's discuss how to influence others.

VISIBILITY ISN'T ABOUT SEEKING THE SPOTLIGHT—IT'S ABOUT LETTING YOUR WORK BE SEEN.

Influencing

Influencing is the ability to impact and even change how someone thinks. It is the ability to bring others around to your way of thinking or at least have an imprint on their thinking. Doing so allows you to affect the decisions at your company and ultimately your career. Successful leaders are able to influence their leaders, colleagues, employees, partners, and shareholders.

When I was a chief of staff for a president of a corporate division at American Express, I had to influence the president's direct reports—all senior vice presidents (SVPs)—to get them to do things they generally deprioritized. I had authority, as they knew I was collecting information for their boss, the president. They did not want to upset their boss, but they also had other important ways to spend their time. I was surprised to learn so early on in my career that SVPs don't always do what their boss tells them to do. Each SVP had a different workstyle, and I learned one SVP in particular needed me to stop by his office to ask him to complete to-dos he was late with. For another, I needed to CC his administrative assistant to get her to put time on his calendar to complete the task. These are examples of understanding your audience and using your knowledge to influence them.

If you want to influence others, you have to think in their terms and build their trust. If something is not working, try something else. To influence a privacy manager to look at my document before all the things on her list, I once went so far as to bake her favorite cookies: chocolate chip. It worked when repeated emails did not. But I would not use that tactic frequently.

SPEAKING UP TO INFLUENCE

In order to influence others, you will need to speak up. Use all the techniques from Chapter 8 in speaking up. You may even have to interrupt someone. Keep focused on your goal to overcome any challenges you face in influencing others.

Research from Brigham Young University showed that speaking up and speaking more is correlated with perceived influence. "Participants who held the floor for a greater percentage of the group's deliberation were more likely to be seen as influential by the other members of the group. Thus, the active use of voice translates into greater perceived influence." Speaking up not only enables you to share your perspective but also creates the perception that you have influence. And when we tie that to visibility, you can be seen as someone with ideas and ability to influence.

A Step-by-Step Process to Influence Others

Influencing requires building trust, having competence, being a strong communicator, and being strategic in how you communicate. Let's review a simple model for influencing others that I learned from one of my earlier bosses, who had developed presentations for a senior leader. I apply this process repeatedly, from big senior leader presentations to important emails where I want to influence someone. It is called the ABCDEs of Communication Model. (I'm not familiar with who developed this model, but I thank whoever created it because it has helped me so much.) I like to call it the ABCDEs of Influence as it is the key to communicating in a way that will most effectively influence others.

Audience – Know who you're talking to.

Behavior Objective – Know what you want them to do, think, and feel.

Content – Say what matters.

Design – Shape it so it sticks.

Evaluation – Ask: Did it work?

Figure 10.1: The ABCDEs of Influence

As shown in Figure 10.1, there are five parts to this framework:

- **Audience**: Define the Audience—to whom you are communicating or trying to influence—with as much detail as you can. How do they consume information? What are their priorities? What is your relationship with this person or people? Define multiple people if there are several.
- **Behavior Objective**: This is the outcome you want. There are usually both a Business Objective as well as a Personal Leadership Objective.
    - Usually, we are pretty clear on the Business Objective, such as getting a decision or getting input. Never identify your Business Objective as simply to update the leader. Think harder. You are updating the person for what purpose? To get input, minimize the chance of the person changing the

plan later, mitigating any risks they may identify? Get specific about a successful outcome of the meeting from a business perspective.

  - Determine your Personal Leadership Objective. What do you want to achieve from a leadership perspective? It could be to be seen as a strategic leader, to build trust, or to be visible because a new job opened up in that person's organization.

- **Content**: What is the Content you need to support the desired Behavior Objective or outcome and what does the audience need/want to make a decision or provide input? If you want a decision, you need to provide the information that person needs to make the decision. List out all the Content you need to achieve your Behavior Objectives.
- **Design**: What is the best Design for your Content based on your Audience and the Behavior Objective? For example, are there lots of charts or graphs or pictures of customers and their stories? Is it verbal or in writing? Is it a conversation or an email or presentation? How you deliver the material will impact your ability to influence. Think of the design based on the preferences of the Audience in addition to the topic. This is also the opportunity to think through what the story is and how to tell it. What conclusions do you want the Audience to walk away with? Remember from Chapter 9 the importance of including stories in your presentation. People are more likely to remember the stories than any of the details of your proposal. Make sure the stories speak to your Audience.
- **Evaluation**: Did you achieve your Behavior Objectives? After the communication, ask yourself what went well and what could have been better. Did you achieve your Personal

Leadership Objective? What is your discernment of success, or is there someone you can ask for feedback? You can certainly do this Evaluation yourself. Sometimes the Business Behavior Objective is clear—you get approval or you do not. Sometimes even that is not clear. And usually, the Personal Leadership Objective is a more nuanced question to assess. So first do your own Evaluation and then look to others to help provide other perspectives.

To help illustrate how all the pieces of the ABCDEs come together, Table 10.2 shows an example based on my need to present a strategic plan to a new senior leader.

A: Audience	My skip leader (Jane) is the main Audience. She is busy and does not have much time. She is analytical and wants to see the numbers and calculations. I don't know her well, so I think she probably does not have a good or bad impression of me. Her priority is the financials. My boss (Mike) will also be at the meeting. He reports to Jane, and he can help persuade her. But he is much more interested in and persuaded by customer stories than the numbers. So my main Audience, Jane, is focused on the numbers, but I also have to think about what Mike is interested in.
B: Behavior Objective	The Business Objective is to approve my plan and the budget. In my scenario, my Personal Leadership Objective is to build a relationship with my new skip leader and have her think of me as a strategic asset.
C: Content	The Content is strategies and budget. Since Jane is very analytical and she is new in her role, she probably wants the last few years of budget numbers, so I must include this. My boss, Mike, on the other hand, wants to hear the customer impact, so I should include customer quotes or customer satisfaction data. And to cover my Personal Leadership Objective of being seen as strategic, I will include the market and competitive analysis in an analytical way.

continued

D: Design	Since this is an important decision, creating a deck and having a discussion is the best Design. An email alone would not enable us to have a conversation and answer her questions, and it would not meet my Personal Behavior Objective of building a relationship with Jane. Jane is new, does not have much time, and is very analytical. So I want to have a one-page executive summary with enough information for her to make a decision, especially as we may not get beyond that first page in the meeting. I will include all the data in the deck and/or in the appendix. To address Mike's interests, I will include a page of customer quotes early in the deck.
E: Evaluation	Since my boss was in the meeting, I can ask him for feedback. Did he think I came across as strategic? I can also evaluate based on results. Were the plan and budget approved? Did I make any progress in building a relationship with Jane?

Table 10.2: Example of the ABCDEs of Influence

Influencing Multiple People

Similar to our discussion on visibility, you can identify all the people you want to influence. This could be the same or a different list for visibility.

A stakeholder map is a way to identify all the people who may have an opinion on or could influence your project or decision. See an example of a stakeholder map in Figure 10.2. When I was working on a change in a privacy policy, I had to make sure the legal department was aligned. I had to get approval from the leaders, including my own. I had to get input and alignment from marketing, sales engineering, and operations through their leadership. But there was also a particular person who had relationships with external privacy organizations. It was important to get this person explicitly on board or our change would likely not be successful internally or externally. I did a pre-meeting with this person to make sure I knew what concerns he had, so I could address them before we got to the bigger meeting. I also identified allies who would help support my proposed changes in the big decision meeting. And I made sure I knew who was likely to object to the changes and addressed their concerns either beforehand or in the content of the presentation.

Think about who on your stakeholder map you need to influence or who might be against your idea and mitigate their concerns.

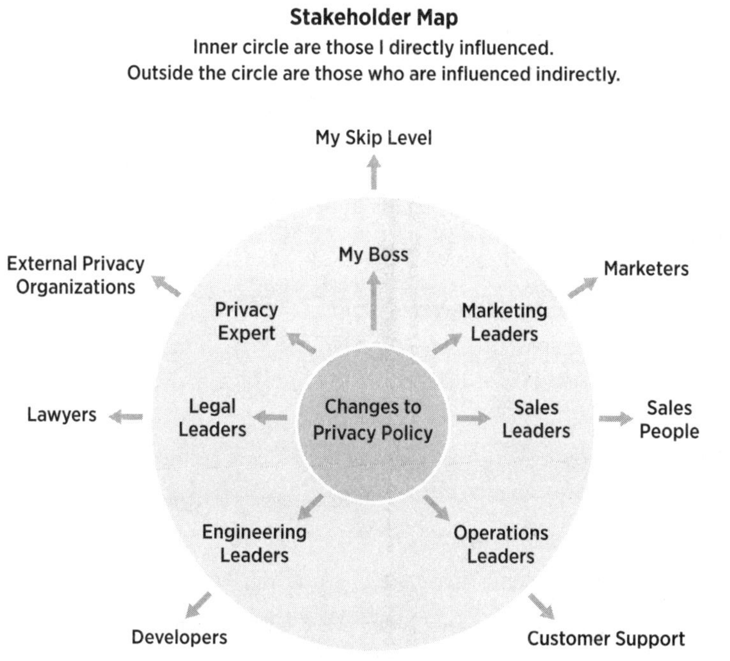

Figure 10.2: Stakeholder map

Moving into the Spotlight

I used to think you had to be an extrovert to influence others. I pictured the charismatic speaker who could speak so fluidly and "sell the socks off" an idea. That is so not me. And I assume you feel the same way. But we as introverts can be highly influential in our own ways. According to *The Introverted Leader* author Jennifer Kahnweiler, "Introverts can be highly effective influencers when they make the most of their own natural strengths instead of trying to act like extroverts." Using your well-thought-out ideas and insights prepared in advance combined with planning can help you put together a cohesive argument that speaks to the audience and addresses concerns. Using your keen observation skills in the meeting, you can identify when someone is agreeing or disagreeing without them even saying a word. Use your strengths to your advantage.

WHAT CAN YOU LEARN ABOUT INFLUENCING FROM EXTROVERTS?

If you are an introvert, your goal is not to become an extrovert. However, you can observe extroverts and what they do to influence others. As Arnie Kozak, author of *The Awakened Introvert*, likes to say, introverts can have "extrovert fascination." Watch how they use their energy, emphasizing a point with a louder voice or standing up to write an idea on a whiteboard. Observe how they use body language; observe their comfort level with speaking and what, precisely, shows they are comfortable. Identify behaviors others are doing that you want to borrow. Experiment to see if it works for you. Again, don't change who you are; just try the behaviors.

You may have a self-limiting belief that you (or introverts in general) cannot be influential or charismatic. That is not true—think about influential introverts like Oprah Winfrey and Warren Buffett. According to *The Irresistible Introvert: Harness the Power of Quiet Charisma* author Michaela Chung, "True charisma has to do with a person's ability to draw us in and hold our attention . . . Once we have reconnected to our inner nature, developing charisma is more about revealing what is already there, rather than adding anything on." Introverts can be charismatic if they can be themselves. So let some of you and your passion come through via stories or an introduction or conclusion. Even if you are not the loud extroverted leader whom everyone notices when you walk into a room, you have the strengths—and now techniques—to influence with the best of them and still remain yourself. Introverts know we need visibility, but it makes us uncomfortable. Hopefully, you have identified ways to be visible in your own way to ensure your strengths and accomplishments are known by the right people. Visibility isn't about seeking the spotlight—it's about letting your work be seen. Your ability to influence is a direct complement to visibility. The ABCDEs of Influence is a formula that can help you formulate your proposals in a way that is most likely to have the impact you want. Influence isn't about pushing your ideas—it's about shaping them for the people who matter. With both visibility and influencing, you can leverage your introverted strengths to be successful in your own personal way, step by step.

INFLUENCE ISN'T ABOUT PUSHING YOUR IDEAS—IT'S ABOUT SHAPING THEM FOR THE PEOPLE WHO MATTER.

ACTIONS TO CONSIDER

If you feel inspired to take action based on this chapter, here are some ideas to get you started.

- Start by thinking about your why: How will being more visible help you? Once you're clear on the why, consider the who, what, and tactics.

continued

- Identify the fears you have about becoming more visible. What is your Critical Voice saying to you? How can you silence that voice?
- If you are not as influential as you would like to be or think you need to be, think about why that may be. Review the ABCDEs of Influence in this chapter for increasing your influence and experiment with it.

Review your *Lead with Quiet Confidence Workbook* at www.JenniferMarcou.com/resources to help you identify your why, your what, and how to gain visibility and influence.

11

Networking: One Conversation at a Time

Networking is a lot like nutrition and fitness: we know what to do, the hard part is making it a top priority.

—Herminia Ibarra

I got my first job out of business school by networking. A friend of mine knew a senior marketing leader at American Express and introduced me to him. While I had to go through all the interviews like everyone else, I'm certain that connection tilted the scale in my favor, and I got the job.

Similarly, I got my job at Microsoft through a former colleague at American Express. My former colleague was not interested in the Microsoft position, but since I had let him know I was looking for roles in Seattle, he forwarded my name on to the recruiter.

Networking works! In fact, according to a 2022 LinkedIn survey, 85 percent of jobs are filled through networking. And according to Sallie

Krawcheck, successful head of Bank of America Wealth Management and now CEO and founder of Ellevest, a digital financial services company for women, "Networking is the No. 1 unwritten rule of success in business."

I've found it a more comfortable situation reaching out to a leader who is hiring through people I know. There have also been hundreds if not thousands of contacts I've made that did not result in a job, but reaching out enabled me to meet new people or learn something new. Not all networking contacts need to result in a specific action. The process itself can be engaging and a learning experience, even for introverts.

Yet the concept of *networking* brings about such dread! It sometimes sends chills up my spine. I know I need to do it. But even with all my networking success, I still imagine it as walking into a ballroom at a conference with a hundred strangers and having to talk to them. Ugh! That sounds horrible! Are you with me?

In this chapter, I'll break down what networking is, why you need to do it, and, most importantly, how to do it on your terms as an introvert. Yes, networking can take the form of a large ballroom of strangers, but fortunately for those of us with introverted preferences, there are a lot of other ways to network.

The Many Facets of Networking

According to the CRM software website www.breakcold.com, "Networking is the intentional act of building relationships with others to exchange information, resources, and support." Seth Godin, author of *Tribes* and *This Is Marketing*, says, "Networking that matters is helping people achieve their goals."

No matter how you view it, networking is a core leadership skill, helping you do the following:

- Identify job opportunities/career advancement (this is probably what most people think of when they think of networking)
- Develop partnerships
- Identify a mentor
- Find investors
- Identify new customers
- Develop new skills
- Make friends
- Help others with your knowledge, connections, experience

Note that last bullet. Networking is a two-way street. It is not just about you taking from one person; it is about sharing and finding the mutual benefit. Earl G. Graves Sr., businessman, entrepreneur, and founder of *Black Enterprise* magazine, said, "What makes networking work is that it sets up win-win situations in which all parties involved get to take something home. Networking is a sharing process. Until you understand that, you won't have much of a network."

Graves's insight is supported by biology. Neuroscience education site Knowing Neurons shares research that concludes "hidden deep within our neural circuits are mechanisms that reward generosity, forge connections, and even ensure our survival. . . . This evolutionary programming explains why helping others often feels so inherently rewarding and meaningful."

As an independent introvert who hates to ask for help, networking became much more palatable to me when I started to view it as a two-way street. Once I appreciated this give-and-take nature of networking, it became less stressful and dreadful. Networking was not about me constantly asking for favors. I realized I could add value to the other person by sharing information or just making them feel good about helping me. With that view, it was clear I was not bothering the American Express colleague who referred me to the Microsoft role by telling him I was looking for roles in Seattle. I got a good referral, and he felt good referring me to an opportunity that came his way. It took him two seconds to forward on the email, and it changed my career trajectory.

Consider this: You may be able to help the other party, so if you don't network, the other party is missing out on your help. So instead of thinking that you are taking the other person's time when you are networking, reframe it: You are giving the gift to that person to be fully present. Your strength of listening is unique in an extroverted world. Appreciate the value of just your presence. And think about the things you can offer to that person: Maybe it's an understanding of the job market or perhaps a great book you have just read.

Different Types of Networking

Despite my nightmare scenario of a ballroom filled with strangers, networking can take many different forms:

- Informational interviews where you schedule time with a hiring leader or someone in an area you are interested in and ask questions about specific jobs and teams
- A casual encounter, such as getting coffee or meeting for lunch, to learn about someone's career trajectory
- Being active on LinkedIn by posting, responding to other posts, finding articles that you can share with your network by reposting or emailing

- Reaching out on LinkedIn and asking for time to learn about someone's company or expertise
- Staying in touch with former colleagues or bosses as you and they move to different roles, companies, and industries
- Creating a personal board of advisors you select for their expertise and style, such as a marketing guru, the person who challenges you, the person who has great empathy, the person you aspire to be. Meet with these individuals periodically or as needed, such as annually or when you are contemplating making career changes.

There are a handful of people I reach out to at least once a year for career advice. And there are others—past bosses or colleagues—I know I could reach out to even if I have not talked to them in several years. It is always easier when you have kept in touch periodically. There is no defined way to network.

BE OPEN TO OPPORTUNITIES AND CONNECTION FROM SURPRISING PLACES

Networking can come from unexpected places. Sometimes an opportunity could come from a friend of a friend or a neighbor you see at the grocery store. Sometimes it comes from a colleague you have not spoken to in five years. Stay open to opportunities. The key is to interact with others on a week-to-week basis outside of your typical work group. If this sounds daunting, I have tips below on what to talk about and how to connect with others in your style.

One Conversation at a Time: Making Networking Less Painful

Now that you appreciate the importance of networking and realize it can take different forms, the question is how do you do it when it goes against every grain in your body?

Meeting new people or being in large groups can be uncomfortable for introverts. But that does not mean we cannot network, as long as we shift our mindset reflected in the title of this chapter: Think of networking as one conversation at a time (Figure 11.1).

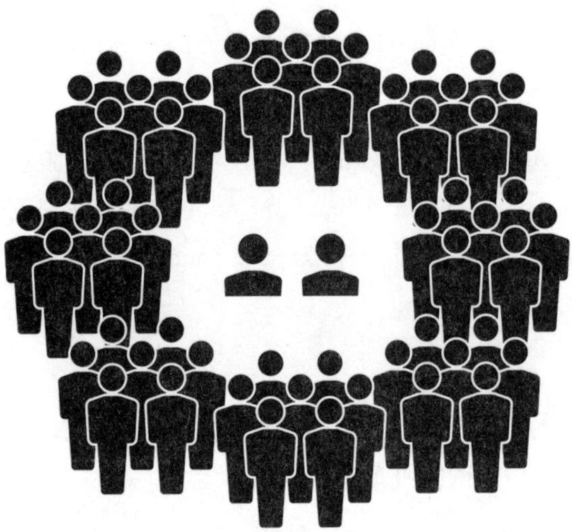

Figure 11.1: Networking is one conversation at a time.

Here are some tips to help you ease into these conversations.

Start Networking with People You Know

Networking does not mean you are calling strangers for a job. In fact, Reid Hoffman, cofounder of LinkedIn, stated, "One of the challenges in networking is everybody thinks it's making cold calls to strangers. Actually, it's the people who already have strong trust relationships with you, who know you're dedicated, smart, a team player, who can help you." Networking starts with people you already know. I now realize this, as many of the jobs in my career started with reaching out to a friend or former colleague or a connection to a connection. So start with the people you know.

Choose Your Best Environment for Networking

The good news is you can choose *how* and *when* to network. Introverts typically do better in one-on-ones or smaller groups, so perhaps choose those types of forums, like having coffee or lunch with someone or joining a smaller industry or trade group. But it can also take place in the large ballrooms of conferences if that is what you like. You can join industry associations, go to conferences, or attend alumni events.

NETWORKING IS ONE CONVERSATION AT A TIME.

If possible, choose the environment to meet with people that is most conducive and comfortable to achieving your objectives. Instead of trying to talk to someone in the hallway spur of the moment, schedule time to speak. Or identify people you want to speak with one-on-one instead of in a large group. Pick quiet places to talk versus loud restaurants or bars. Obviously, there will be times when you won't be able to control whether you are in a large group or loud situation. Nonetheless, do your best to try to influence making it more comfortable for you. You can say things like, "Let's move away from the bar to the table where it is quieter" or "Do you mind if we take a walk outside to get some fresh air?" Try to make it as effective as possible for you.

Approach Individuals or Small Groups

When I focus on meeting one or two people at a time—even in a crowded ballroom—networking seems less overwhelming. Usually, I approach people who look friendly, those who are smiling or acknowledging my presence. If the person is in a group, I listen before I jump into the conversation. But I do try to add some comment to the topic or ask a question in the first couple of minutes.

At lunch during a large conference, I try to approach someone who is sitting alone (and not reading) instead of going to the boisterous table. I figure they like solitude, so perhaps we can have a quiet one-one-one talk.

If I am targeting an individual I want to have a one-on-one with, I ask for time on their calendar, stating specifically what I am looking for, such as advice on moving to their department or learning how they made the jump to senior manager. Then I come prepared with questions to ask or topics I want to learn about.

Volunteer for Projects/Groups That Expose You to New People

Enhancing your visibility, which we discussed in the last chapter, and networking can be done at the same time in a noninvasive way. For example, you can speak about your area of expertise in a lunch-and-learn or even get on your company's internal website to share a question, comment, or observation. Getting involved in employee or business resource groups is also beneficial because you can choose what you want to participate in and tailor your networking activities to your interests. For instance, maybe the newest innovations in tech appeal to you more than a group focused on working moms. These ideas enable you to meet people outside of your direct working groups but are still in line with your expertise or areas of interest.

Conversation Tips for Introverts

During these "one conversation at a time" events, what should you talk about? The answer is usually clear if you have a specific goal in mind, such as finding a job opportunity or learning about a specific topic. But if you don't have a goal or don't know what you don't know, get curious and ask questions. Curiosity can spark positive feelings in the brain to make networking seem less stressful. According to *The Introvert's Way* author Sophia Dembling, "Small talk connects us and greases the gears of society."

Here are some strategies for starting (and continuing) a conversation:

Get the Other Person to Talk (Be Curious)

Get the other person to tell their story. I have found as an introvert I hate to talk about myself, so I have become very good at asking questions in conversations. I ask open-ended questions to get them to tell their story, such as what they do and how they got into that role.

Smile and Nod at People More

How many times have I been told I have a poker face and people can't tell what I am thinking? Smiling is a simple but powerful gesture to connect to others without even speaking. Extroverts love getting smiles, as it gives them a dopamine hit, and it takes very little of your energy to execute. So nod your head more as you're listening. Extroverts will pick up on the positive feedback, and it will also keep them talking so you don't have to.

Steer the Conversation to Areas You Want to Talk About or Learn

Besides asking questions and sharing about yourself, you can identify what you enjoy talking about. It could be movies, books, sports, cooking. These can be safe topics in which you can ask questions and freely share your perspective. My go-to is, "What TV shows have you recently watched and would recommend?" as I am always looking for my next binge-watch.

Use Your Introvert Strengths

Preparation, listening, and observation are superpowers of introverts, so use them to your advantage. Several of the previous ideas revolve around preparing what you want to talk about or what questions you want to ask. You can also use your powerful listening skills. You can stand there passively and listen, or you can listen intently and get beyond the words that are said. Go deeper by asking "why" questions, which will get them talking beyond just surface facts.

Use your powers of observation. Focus on your senses: What do you see, hear, feel? And use that information to guide you toward whom you want to talk to or what action you want to take. For instance, I tend to gravitate toward people on the outside of the room who are alone, as they seem less intimidating to start a conversation with. You can also observe extroverted people and learn how they interact. Take any ideas you want to experiment with in your next networking experience.

Prepare to Share About Yourself

In a traditional networking situation where you don't know the other person, be prepared to answer the "tell me about yourself" prompt. It may feel like an interview, so share only details that you feel comfortable with. You can even have a thirty-second description of who you are prepared in advance. It is like your own personal elevator pitch. This can be modified depending on your objective—whether it's finding a job, finding a tennis partner, or learning about something.

DEVELOP A SUCCINCT DESCRIPTION OF WHAT YOU DO

Because the question "what do you do?" is so common in networking situations, I advise that you develop and practice using a brief description that you can rattle off without stumbling.

For example, I worked with my coaching client Sandra to say, "I help customers save time by designing easy-to-use software." She is a user experience specialist at a software company, and instead of using lots of technical jargon, she focused on the real customer benefit of what she did and boiled it down to eleven words. And there is enough ambiguity in her statement that it piques someone's curiosity to ask questions: What software? How do you make it easy to use? These questions continue the conversation and enable her to share comfortably the details of what she does without feeling like she is self-promoting.

Dare to Be Honest and Vulnerable

Even if it doesn't feel like it, people want to learn more about you. Identify the details of what you want to share. Sometimes being a little vulnerable ends up creating a powerful connection. This does not need to be opening up about everything in your life. But identify an area that you may be open to share. For instance, at one business lunch, I started to talk to someone who was also not talking to anyone else in the buffet line and said, "I am an introvert, and I hate these things." She felt the same way and we immediately connected. We spent maybe five minutes chatting in line, but it was such a deep and energizing conversation about how she felt and deals with those situations. We were then secret comrades as introverts in that extroverted environment.

Identify Conversational Boundaries

Though vulnerability helps people connect with you, that doesn't mean you have to bare your soul. Identify your boundaries: things you want to talk about and things you do *not* want to talk about. Perhaps it is not wanting to talk about your family or marital status or a private passion. Just make your own personal list and know that you don't want to talk about these things. If someone asks you about it, be prepared for how you want to politely respond. For example, if someone asks, "Do you have kids?" you can say, "I have a dog" or "I prefer not to talk about my personal life" and shift it to something you are comfortable talking about, like "What are you working on?"

This strategy worked well for Cali, a project manager at a medical device company. She was attending a cocktail hour for work and found the noise of people talking in the bar giving her a headache. Her colleague John asked how she was doing. She really wanted to say, "Horrible," and leave. But instead, she said, "Good." And then the uncomfortable conversational silence began. John turned and engaged with someone else. Another colleague, Sarah, said she had to leave to go to her kid's soccer game. "Do you have kids?" Sarah asked. The dreaded question! Cali and her husband had been going through infertility treatments for a year with no success. Questions about family seemed deeply personal, and she was never sure how to answer. She gave a quick no, and Sarah seemed disappointed. Cali asked where the restroom was.

Interacting with her colleagues and strangers in social situations is required for Cali to be successful in her job, as she has to build relationships across departments to be a successful project manager and for her to be recommended to new projects. Why did these events seem so awkward, personal, and exhausting? Why couldn't Cali just do her job and not have to attend these uncomfortable events? And these were her colleagues—people she worked with. It was even worse when she had to talk to strangers at trainings and conferences. She couldn't stand talking about the weather. It's not that she couldn't talk to people; it's that she preferred to go deeper on topics in quiet places with just one or two people. Cali realized she needed to find strategies to survive these situations, because she wanted to be a sought-after project manager within her group.

Together, Cali and I created a list of topics she was comfortable talking about, which included dogs, sports, and art. Then we prepared a response to questions she did not feel comfortable talking about, like "No, I don't have kids, but I love dogs" or "I grew up in North Dakota, but I love living in California now. I especially love beach volleyball." Soon, large gatherings became less anxiety provoking.

At the next work cocktail hour, David, her manager, called her over and said, "Cali, meet James, the new marketing manager." Cali responded, "So nice to meet you. Where are you from?" After James shared his background, he asked her, "What do you do for fun on the weekends?" Cali responded, prepared and without the normal hesitation, "I love the local art museum. There is an exhibit on Monet through September. I also love walking my dog on the beach. What do you like to do for fun?" Cali was off and running, sharing about herself with the boundaries she had set up and with prepared topics. She was actually having fun meeting a new colleague. She felt much more confident and comfortable going into group events. And the next month, when she started working with James on a project, they more quickly worked collaboratively and productively, as they had started the connection at that work event.

Getting Started

For me, the hardest part of networking is always how to start a one-on-one conversation. The difference in my approach depends on whether I'm talking to a complete stranger I know nothing about (and therefore have no specific goal in mind) or someone I've purposefully selected to talk to.

Talking to Complete Strangers

If I don't have a specific person to target or goal to achieve, I catch someone's eye, smile, and then make a comment about our current environment: "Great food," or "Interesting program," or "Good to see so many colleagues." Then I move onto an opening question. This is my strategy to pass the conversation ball to the other person. An opener could be about the conference or event you are at:

- What is your favorite part of this conference?
- What have you learned so far?
- What sessions do you recommend?

Or it could be about what the person is working on or doing:

- What are you working on?
- What are your plans this weekend? This summer?

Or it could be an observation about the situation:

- Have you noticed how few women are here? (if you are both women)
- Have you noticed how engaged everyone has been? Or quiet?

Think about what you'd like to learn from that person. Focus on what is interesting to you. Here are other questions that can help you learn about a person and find a commonality:

- What's your favorite thing to do on weekends?
  - Build on that question if there is something in common—e.g., "I love to read as well—what are you reading now?"
- What's your favorite restaurant around here?
- What is the biggest challenge you are facing right now?
- What brought you to this event?

Sometimes I think about a specific purpose I have in talking to these strangers, like I want to learn something new about another company or an area within my company. Or I want to find a new book to read. Or I want to find a friendly face to go with to the group dinner that night. I have had clients who set goals of talking to three new people at every large event. Identifying a goal can be a way to focus on a purpose versus the seemingly random nature of meeting large groups of people.

Talking to a Specific Person

For situations where there is a particular person I want to talk to, I try to be specific about my objective (e.g., learning about an opportunity or sharing something about yourself). Here are some examples:

- What do you do? How did you get into that? What do you want to do going forward?
- Can you tell me more about X?
- I have a background in X and I want to get into Y. Do you have any recommendations about where to learn more or who to meet?

And in most conversations, if you are information seeking, you may want to ask:

- Is there anyone else you think I should talk to about X or getting into company Y?

This can create a chain of new contacts.

Building a Networking Foundation

"Because I am supposed to" is not a sufficient reason to network. That's why I encourage people to think about why they want to network: Networking will become easier if you tie it to a specific goal that is personal *for you* versus "shoulding" all over yourself.

That said, building relationships *before* you need them will make people more willing to help you, and you will feel less needy as you will have likely provided value to that contact through your ongoing interactions. For that reason, I advise everyone to develop a plan or approach for networking that they use regularly to establish or maintain connections. What that looks like will vary greatly from person to person. Here are just a few possibilities:

- Setting a goal of meeting one new person a month for coffee
- Reconnecting with former colleagues a couple times a year to stay in touch
- Targeting people in a certain industry or company to meet (such as someone you want to hire you!)
- Meeting people in a broad variety of areas through volunteer work, family or friends, online groups, book clubs, and much more

When I was looking for a job in Seattle after living in New York, I wanted to let people know about my desired move in case they had ideas or contacts. Getting a job in Seattle, where I was moving, was my why. I let my network know through emails and LinkedIn posts. It didn't feel like networking to me, but it was.

Now, when a new coach reaches out to me for advice, I will always meet with them, as I know there is likely some way I can help them. And most times, there is something I learn that can help me. My why in meeting with coaches is to help them, with an extra benefit of learning something new myself. And it also works in reverse: If I am looking for continuing-education classes, I reach out to my coaching network for a vetted list to explore.

WHY YOU SHOULDN'T ALWAYS AIM FOR THE TOP

Many people think that networking is only helpful if they are talking to the most senior person they can reach. This is not true. First, it may be difficult to get time with senior leaders, and second, they may not be the best people to share the details of what you are looking for. Perhaps someone at your same level or just a level above would be more helpful to understand a job or work environment. A more senior person can certainly provide broad and long-term perspective, but they may not know the details of a job. The person at your level or even lower can provide perspective that leaders at a higher level can't, like what the culture is really like, or what the boss's leadership style is.

Networking One Contact at a Time: Carol's Story

Carol, a marketing manager at a financial services company, wanted to find a new job in her company but hated networking. She did not know many people outside of her department. She used the LEAD with Quiet Confidence Framework to identify actions around networking.

Learn: She picked the learning objective of meeting people in a department she was interested in learning about.

Experiment: Her experiment was to ask people she knew in her department for recommendations for people to talk to in her targeted department. She wanted to identify two people to start. (Originally, she said five, but that seemed too hard. Two was a Kind goal.) Once she got their names, she sent them an email asking for thirty minutes of their time or to go to coffee. She prepared the questions she wanted to ask.

Assess: She got one immediate response and scheduled a coffee that went well. She got better insight into the other group and wanted to learn more. She never heard back from the other contact, which did not bother her as much as she imagined. She guessed that the other person was probably busy. She celebrated her action by getting her favorite strawberry mango protein smoothie after her first networking conversation. She was glad she got the first one done.

She realized it was not as hard as she'd thought it would be. People are very willing to share, especially when talking about themselves. And she felt less nervous when she asked people she knew for contacts versus cold-calling people. Preparing her questions ahead of time enabled her to focus on what the other person said versus what she was going to ask next.

Develop: She was excited about what she had learned and had asked the first contact, "Who else should I talk to?" The first contact recommended a colleague who had more experience in the department and had a similar background to Carol. So she reached out to schedule time. This time she was less nervous about sending the email.

She also decided to find two more people to reach out to from her existing colleagues. She said to herself, *Carol, you've got this.*

If you still feel reticent to network, think about what is holding you back. Perhaps a visit to your Wisdom Within, addressing your Critical Voice, or reframing networking as helping others can help break the barriers.

Networking with Less Stress

Networking does not need to be stressful. It is simply an exchange of information between two people, a give-and-take. Introverts can be successful networkers if they approach it in their way. You can approach it in ways that work best for you. Identify why you want to network. Start with people you know and are comfortable with. Prepare questions and comments. Get curious. Use your introvert strengths of listening, observing, and desiring to go deeper. You will likely have to face situations that are not optimal, such as walking into large groups of strangers or loud situations. But you can use your personal tool kit of strategies to network successfully even in those situations. When you are networking, you need to "say it (share your thoughts/ask your questions), send it (send the email invite), show up (as yourself at the event or meeting)." It's just one conversation at a time.

ACTIONS TO CONSIDER

If you feel inspired to take action based on this chapter, here are some ideas to get you started.

- Start by thinking about your why: What do you want to accomplish with networking? Do you have an immediate need or are you establishing a foundation?
- What actions are you already taking that would count as networking? What could you do to expand on those?
- What are your biggest fears around networking? Which of the strategies in Chapter 7 can you use to silence those inner Critical Voices?
- Pick *one* event you're going to attend in the near future and develop a plan for networking at that event. Use the LEAD with Quiet Confidence Framework. Prepare questions you can ask of others. Think about your boundaries

continued

and how to politely redirect the conversation. What is a realistic goal?

The *Lead with Quiet Confidence Workbook* at www.JenniferMarcou.com/resources can help you capture your thoughts and things you want to consider in your networking plans.

12

Managing Your Energy

With a charged social battery, an introvert is indistinguishable from an extrovert—it's what they do afterward, when they are tired, that differentiates them. If you see someone who appears to be shy or unapproachable, chances are they are simply socially tapped out.

—Peter Hollins

The lights are flashing, explosions are happening on big screens, different rock songs are blaring all around me, and the convention center hall is packed with people talking and playing first-person shooter video games. I am at the Electronic Entertainment Expo (E3 for short), the largest and ultimate video gaming conference; it is a high point for marketing video games.

On top of all this, I have to socialize with my colleagues all day and every evening. I go to the "quietest" corner of the showroom and play a game of sorting crabs that mirrors the TV show *Deadliest Catch*. This game is certainly not making headlines like Xbox's premiere game, but it is a way to participate in the conference despite being in an environment that strains the limits of my mental and physical capacity.

I was the director of digital marketing for Xbox, and it was an honor to be selected to attend. I have a headache and want to go back to my hotel room and stay there for the rest of the three-day conference. But I am new to the gaming industry and have a lot to learn. I realize I have a dream job, but it is someone else's dream job, not mine.

I return home exhausted. It was just too overwhelming, and I was unable to manage my time alone to reenergize since I was constantly being pulled by my colleagues to go to the presentations, visit the booths, and attend all the after-hour parties.

When I return to the office, I tell my boss I would rather quit than go to that conference again. He said he understood and knew there were plenty of other team members who wanted to go. But I think it was hard for him to empathize, as his extroverted self thrived in the busy, noisy E3 environment. Fortunately for me, attendance at the E3 is not a requirement of my job, and I was able to stay in the marketing director role for three successful years without having to go back to E3 or any other gaming conference.

This may be an extreme example, but introverts face challenges every day doing things that suck our energy. As we learned in Chapter 2, our introverted brains work differently than extroverted brains. Our brains are working much harder to observe, analyze, and interpret signals all around us, so interactions with people, particularly multiple people at once, can be very taxing for us introverts. In addition, our brains are less dependent on dopamine from human interactions, so meeting with lots of people is not always rewarding like it is for extroverts. And on top of all of that, our brains are functioning at a higher activation rate.

INTROVERTS DON'T LACK ENERGY—WE JUST SPEND IT DIFFERENTLY.

No wonder we are exhausted after a long day of meetings, team-building gatherings, or networking events. Introverts don't lack energy—we just spend it differently.

That's why another skill that introverts need to master is energy management. Without that skill, we may have a hard time doing all the other things we need to do to be perceived as an effective leader: speaking up, having an executive presence, making sure we are visible, and networking. In this chapter, I'll dive more deeply into the topic of energy management and provide practical tips for developing a strategy that will work for you.

Why Introverts Need Time Alone

From our original definition of *introversion*, the issue is not that introverts cannot socialize and connect with people; it is that introverts need time to recover from those interactions to be most effective and authentically themselves. Introverts get energy by being alone.

There is also a high correlation between highly sensitive people (people who are more sensitive to sound, light, touch, taste, smell) and introversion. So not only do people who are both introverted and highly sensitive need time alone to reenergize, they are also quickly overtaxed by too much stimulation.

A day full of meetings is exhausting. Add on an evening social event and introverts are maxed out. According to PsychCentral, "[I]ntroverts need more quiet, alone time. This allows them to think things through and plan. Not finding the time or opportunity to engage in thought and mentally cope with everyday stressors on your own way may increase your stress levels."

In short, we need time without people to recenter. Quiet and solitude allow our brains to settle from a highly activated state. Arnie Kozak, author of *The Awakened Introvert*, says the purpose of solitude is to "reconnect with your sense of quiet, values, and intentions." It allows you to recharge your batteries.

Many introverts may wonder whether they could live a life without interacting with other people. I, in fact, had a fantasy when I was in high school that all human brains could be connected to each other with wires to share ideas, but we would not have to actually interact in real life. It was a strange fantasy, but points to the core need to not spend an inordinate amount of time with people. (I have since appreciated the importance of human connection and do not avoid it, but I still appreciate that earlier thought.)

The reality is that human connection is important. Scientists at Brigham Young University and University of North Carolina at Chapel Hill found that quality friendship is as important to health as exercise and stopping smoking. So whether we introverts like it or not, to live healthy lives we need to interact with others. But we can plan the who, how, and why of how we interact, and the choices will be different for each one of us.

Developing Your Own Energy Strategy

Developing your own unique strategy for managing your energy has to start with understanding what drains your energy and what gives you energy (what I call energy drainers and gainers). See Figure 12.1.

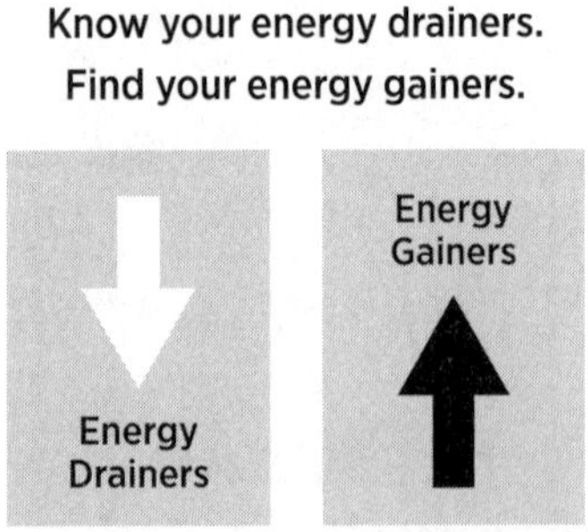

Figure 12.1: Energy drainers and gainers

Identify Your Energy Drainers

Knowing what drains your energy will help you avoid and prepare for those times. For me, back-to-back meetings, large in-person groups where I don't know many people, or a conversation topic that I don't care about drain me.

Henry David Thoreau in *Walden* talks about having a "broad margin" in his life, meaning a simple life, sitting in nature, listening to the birds, and allowing a lapse of time as the sun rises, then sets. How do you create broad margins in your life?

When I was in the corporate world, I color-coded calendar events in red that were stressful or for which I had to present—it got my attention. I could then make sure I kept free time before and after those periods to both prepare and recover. I have several clients who do the same, and it helps them identify when they will need more self-care on a particular day or week.

Start by making a list of what drains you or even look at your calendar for the week. What plans do you see that make you feel exhausted just knowing they are in the offing?

Identify Your Energy Gainers

On the other end of the spectrum, what gives you energy? For me, it is going for a walk by myself and looking out to nature, particularly at an old pine tree outside my office window. Closing my eyes and taking three deep breaths, in through my nose and out through my mouth. Reading a book that I love. Seeing a close friend with whom I can have a deep conversation, not superficial chitchat. Dancing to '80s New Wave music. Having dinner with my family and getting the lowdown on their days.

In the color-coding of my calendar, I colored mentoring sessions in cool, calm green because those were energizers. I could see what in my week would give me energy. The color-coding helped me quickly assess whether it was going to be a tough week, requiring me to add in more energizers, or a relatively calm week.

Make a list of energy boosters for you. Select some you can do at work and some you can do at home.

Develop a Plan for Known Events

When you're aware of your energy drainers, you can plan, monitor your energy level, and be flexible in finding recovery time. Take a look at your calendar for the next week or month. Consider using a color-coding plan like I do. What known energy drainers do you have to participate in? For each one, think about what you can do before, during, and after the event to incorporate your energy gainers. Here are some example strategies I've used:

- **Preparing for an energy-draining event**: If I have an important meeting with lots of people that I know will be an energy drainer, I prepare. I read the agenda and prepare my thoughts. If I am presenting, I practice my presentation so I go in with confidence. Right before the meeting, I take five minutes to do mindful breathing, look at a tree outside my window, or imagine my Wisdom Within and how she would show up in the meeting. What can help *you* relax and/or reenergize *before* an energy drainer?

CREATING A MENTAL GREEN ROOM

Have you heard the term "green room" before? It's a physical room that celebrities or performers spend time in right before they go on stage. It is usually stocked with their favorite food and drink, flowers, music—whatever they need to help them relax and prepare for their performance.

While few of us will have the luxury of having a real green room, it can help to create a mental picture of what yours would look like and to spend time there in your mind before an energy-draining event. What is your ideal green room? Where are you? What items are there? What could you do to relax and stay calm before you have to "perform"?

For me, I am alone in a quiet space, looking at nature. And maybe my Wisdom Within is there encouraging me and/or shooing my Critical Voice away.

- **During an event, what can you do to manage your energy?** I try to stay present, focus on my senses like we learned in Chapter 5, and definitely take a deep breath. If my Critical Voice shows up, I try to actively shift to my Wisdom Within. I try to engage with others to direct the conversation to something that gives me energy, such as getting to a decision in a meeting, exploring a new idea, or talking about something that is meaningful to me. I reconnect with my purpose and what I want to get out of the meeting. What are ideas you have for maintaining energy in a meeting or engagement?
- **What can you do after the event to regain the energy you expended?** I try to schedule a break after a potentially stressful or energy-depleting event, so I have time to myself. Again, being in nature and doing breathing exercises helps me. Exercise also releases my stress and gives me energy. And sometimes it is just doing something I enjoy, like eating a piece of chocolate or watching a favorite show.

Coping Strategies If You Can't Control Your Calendar

Many times, you don't own your time, particularly at work. All-day meetings with attached social events that are expected to have full attendance can be gut-wrenching for introverts to experience.

If you do have to attend more events than you want, make sure you build in energy gainers throughout the day. For instance, at breaks or during lunch, find a quiet space to be by yourself. Go outside and take a walk alone. Reading on your phone or even visiting the bathroom can give you a critical five to ten minutes to yourself. Reward yourself at the end of the day for getting through energy-draining events. For example, you can go for a run, read your book, watch your favorite show, or just sit and do nothing.

If there is a weeklong event, pick and choose what you will attend or skip, so you can manage your energy throughout the week. If all-day off-sites include evening drinks or dinner, decide ahead of time what you want to do. Skip the evening activities or go one night but not the other. Make an appearance—show up for the first fifteen to twenty minutes. If you have to attend something and you don't want to, set a goal such as talking to at least one new person or giving yourself permission to just observe and not actively participate (if that is possible). Make a plan beforehand, so you know when you are close to the end.

Even better would be to give feedback to the event organizer to schedule breaks and not have events in the evening, if possible. Talk to the organizer of off-sites beforehand to make sure everyone can participate in their best capacity. People who have traveled from different time zones or people who need to get home for personal obligations may also be less comfortable with additional evening activities. So you are not alone. Share your voice not just for you but for others who may have similar concerns.

Ongoing Energy Management

Sometimes, the everyday events of life are enough to drain our introvert energy, and we can benefit from having a plan for how we can continually rebuild our energy. Arnie Kozak, author of *The Awakened Introvert*, calls this a "quiet plan." I used to work late on Friday nights when no one was around because I could get so much done without interruptions and feel unburdened as I went into the weekend. I did not feel I needed to work Sunday night to catch up on emails as my colleagues did. It was very freeing and energizing.

Kozak also recommends creating your own social calculator. For each invitation, ask yourself the following questions:

- Do I have the energy to attend this event?
- What is the benefit?
- How important is this event to me—or to people important in my life?
- How can I make it less taxing?
- How will I recover?

You can also consider what your purpose is in attending the event. If it connects with your Purpose (big *P*), then you may be more likely to attend and find it less depleting than if it is not connected to your Purpose. This is a great gauge to see if you want to attend and help you plan for recovery.

I suggest you schedule only as many social events in a week that you can handle. Say no to others. Just because you have a day free for yourself does not mean you have to feel obligated to accept any invitation that comes your way. If you say no and they ask what you are doing, just say you have other plans. Remember, saying no to an invitation means saying yes to protecting your time alone so you can reenergize.

Give yourself permission to have down time. So many clients have told me they feel guilty taking a day or even an afternoon off work to recover. But we all know what that can lead to—burn out. If you have not recovered, you are not going to perform at your best. Lack of sleep can have the same impact on your cognitive abilities as drinking alcohol. To show up as your best self, your best worker, you need rest. Give yourself empathy and make the time for that rest and recovery—even if it is a short walk outside.

SAYING NO TO AN INVITATION MEANS SAYING YES TO PROTECTING YOUR TIME ALONE SO YOU CAN REENERGIZE.

Take Janet, for example. She's a busy lawyer at a financial services company who understood the power of doing nothing to recover from her workday. Her family noticed her sitting on the couch doing literally nothing—no TV, no book—and thought it was strange. But she explained to them she felt so much more energized after sitting for ten minutes in stillness, which enabled her to focus on her family after that quiet time. Her family got used to it, especially because they reaped the benefits of her increased focus and reduced stress at dinner.

Dealing with Disruptions

It's a fact: Your quiet plan will get disrupted! Your boss sends an urgent text you need to respond to; a colleague stops by to ask an impromptu question; an email takes longer to write than you expected; a family member gets sick. So be prepared to adjust on the fly. Identify an alternate time to reenergize or ratchet down the energy you are expending at the moment. What do you do or feel when you are out of energy? I stop talking altogether. I don't care about whatever is being discussed or what I am working on. My eyes get heavy. I feel sluggish. I know in those moments I need a break. Be aware of the signs indicating that you need to reenergize and recover. This awareness will be an important indicator to take the next step—identifying a way to recover *right now.*

Being flexible in identifying things you can do in the moment when you are losing energy will help you recover. Plan ahead by creating a list of actions you can implement in the moment. Maybe it's taking a deep breath in a boring meeting, taking a walk outdoors after the meeting, petting an animal, seeing nature, or drinking water. Mindful breathing and using your senses, such as savoring some hot tea—the taste, the smell, the feeling of the heat of the cup—can work as well. Identify a list of quick things you can do during or right after the taxing event, even if it is not officially on your schedule. Our bodies usually tell us; we just need to listen to them.

With planning and the ability to act on the fly to protect and recover energy, we can be happier and much more effective. Kozak states, "There is an end to introvert-anguish when you can self-empower through insights, self-care, and setting limits on extrovert demands."

Communicating Your Needs for Solitude

There is a lack of understanding from well-intentioned friends, family, and colleagues of the need for introverts to be alone. They engage in lots of cajoling to get us to attend social events or multiple activities on the weekend. It is exhausting to hear about and have to decline. Or sometimes we end up going and regretting it. Being clear on what you want to do and when you want to do it is important. Then you can respond clearly to the invitation and remain true to yourself. I often say, "I can't make it, but thank you for including me." They don't know I can't make it because I was planning to reenergize by reading all afternoon.

Janet, whose story I told above, was forthright in explaining to her family why she needed to sit on the couch "doing nothing." Here's another example: Donna, a senior technical leader at a biomedical company, told colleagues outright that she was an introvert and that the best way to work with her was via email. She was happy to meet in person, as long as the agenda was prepared ahead of time. She preferred to not have all-day meetings, so she would request that off-sites be planned for half of the day over multiple days versus all-day sessions. She was in a position to dictate and influence the design of meetings. But even if you don't have that level of influence and power, you can still share the best way to work with you, such as stating that meeting at five p.m. will not enable you to be at your best. Be transparent about your needs. Remember, half the world is introverted, so there are likely others who would benefit from your requests for optimal meeting design and scheduling.

Saying No to Invitations

To manage your energy effectively, you as an introvert will have to turn down invitations. Saying no is another key skill for introverted leaders. It can feel uncomfortable because you don't want to disappoint or hurt others who are well meaning. Here are some graceful ways to say no from Jenn Granneman from her book *The Secret Lives of Introverts*:

- Respond with a no and "Thank you so much for thinking of me."
- Say no fast and up front.
- Propose alternatives. "I can't do something all day Saturday, but I could do dinner on Monday night."

- Don't budge even when pestered. This can be hard, but you may regret it if you give in.

Take away some of the guilt of saying no by being prepared to say no and taking control of the situation.

Practicing a "Gracious No": Scarlett's Story

Scarlett, a marketing manager for a large tech company, would experience stress on Thursday afternoons because that's when text messages would arrive from colleagues asking what she was doing Friday night. She knew no matter how she answered, her colleagues wanted to see her for drinks and dinner at the end of the week. She felt she could not just say no, knowing she would get pushback if she said she wasn't doing anything (the truth), nor could she say she was doing something else, as her close colleagues would ask to join her. In her mind, there was no way out. She also did not want to look weird to her colleagues or be unkind.

We worked on responses to their invitations that were honest, clear, and also conveyed that she did want to spend time with them periodically. For example, she'd reply, "No, I can't have dinner on Friday night, but let's have drinks on Tuesday." She found she could control the length of time with her colleagues if she suggested something—lunch or drinks—that was faster and more time-bound than dinner. With her newfound confidence to say no without lying or feeling like a loner, she no longer loathed the "What are you doing this Friday?" texts. She found clarity in identifying what she really wanted to do and confidence to tell or redirect others. She still sometimes agrees to go to Friday dinner with colleagues, but she is now consciously saying yes instead of agreeing by default and regretting it.

Using Your Energy Wisely

Everyone needs to manage their energy, but introverted brains in particular need quiet time to reduce stimulation from interactions with others. Introverts can be aware of what energizes them and what depletes them and then create a game plan to energize and recover. Given that 50 percent of the world is introverted, asking for what you need in terms of quiet time or breaks not only helps you but can help others by creating a social norm that it is OK to say no. Know your energy drainers and find your energy gainers to show up authentically you.

KNOW YOUR ENERGY DRAINERS AND FIND YOUR ENERGY GAINERS.

ACTIONS TO CONSIDER

If you feel inspired to take action based on this chapter, here are some ideas to get you started.

- Identify your energy drainers and gainers.
- Get in the habit of planning decompression (energy-gaining time) into your calendar.
- If you have what you anticipate will be a stressful event in the near future, think through steps you can take to prepare ahead of time. How can you show up and stay energized?
- Practice saying no. If possible, offer an alternative time to meet with the person or people under conditions you will find more favorable (limited attendance, limited time, etc.). Practice telling others how you will work most effectively.

- List out your energy drainers and gainers in the *Lead with Quiet Confidence Workbook* at www.JenniferMarcou.com/resources to help better manage your energy.

Part III Tool Review

Tools for Changing Behavior While Staying Authentic

- Use the OARS model to help you gain confidence in speaking up.
  - Open-ended questions
  - Affirmations
  - Reflective listening
  - Summarize
- If you are blindsided or feeling stuck, ask the "anytime" questions (such as "What is our objective here?" or "What do we want to achieve in this meeting?").
- Implement Madeleine Albright's advice for being heard (speak up first, don't bury your head in note-taking, etc.).
- Practice the 3Cs of executive presence.
  - Build your **confidence** through preparation (mental and physical) and practice.
  - Practice effective **communication** (be clear about points you want to make, tell relevant stories, practice your presentations, focus at the right level).

    - Remind yourself of your **competence** (experience, knowledge, etc.).
- Develop a visibility plan—define why, what, who.
- Use the ABCDEs of Influence to more effectively communicate and increase your influence.
    - Audience (use a stakeholder map to identify the different people you need to reach and why and identify what is important to them)
    - Behavior Objectives (business and personal leadership objectives)
    - Content
    - Design
    - Evaluation
- Develop the attitude that networking or social events are "one conversation at a time."
    - Be curious about the person you're talking to.
    - Prepare to share something about yourself.
    - Identify your boundaries and practice strategies for steering the conversation to topics you are comfortable talking about.
- Prior to networking or social events, develop a plan.
    - Identify your energy drainers and energy gainers and have a plan for balancing them out.
    - Color-code your calendar to help you manage drainers and gainers.
    - Identify simple ways to gain energy if you don't have much time or space (deep breaths, short walks, etc.).
- Develop strategies for saying no.

PART IV

IMPACT:
Turning Insight into Implementation

The time has come for you to bring it all together and identify the behaviors you want to change without changing who you are.

In Chapter 13, I'll use examples from my clients to show that introvert leadership is possible, whether you're just starting out with your career or wanting to make a leap up the organizational ladder. Then in Chapter 14, I'll walk you through steps for visualizing how you will grow and progress in your own career, drawing on your internal resources to define a path that will work for you.

Imagine the increased impact, confidence, and success you will have! Envision the balance and happiness you will find. It's up to you to take the first step.

13

Start from Where You Are

In any given moment we have two options:
to step forward into growth or step back into safety.
—Abraham Maslow

I know from my own experience and that of many other introverts I've encountered that the tools and insights covered in the previous chapters can help people at all levels. We can all exhibit confidence and leadership traits, no matter our official positions or job titles. In this chapter, I want to share four client stories that support this belief, including that of a software specialist who wanted to get more confident in his job, a product manager who wanted to gain more influence, a person on the verge of managing others (having direct reports for the first time), and a more senior leader who was struggling in a new leadership position. In each case, the client used tools taught in this book to get out of their comfort zone to "say it, send it, show up" and had significant impact on their career and their life.

Confidence in Speaking with Someone New: Raj's Story

Raj was a senior applications specialist at a biotech firm and was responsible for managing and supporting the software applications in the organization. He frequently had to work with new people, such as customers or external partners, which made him uncomfortable. In fact, every time Raj had a call scheduled with a new customer, he would feel sick to his stomach. He wouldn't sleep well the night before. He felt like he could not perform at his best. He wanted to stop the anxiety of meeting and talking with new people.

SAY IT, SEND IT, SHOW UP.

Raj came to me for help. I prodded to determine what was holding him back. He realized it was his own Critical Voice inside, which we learned about in Chapter 7. He feared that customers and colleagues who did not know him were going to think he was stupid, not adding value to the conversation, or wasting their time.

As soon as we went through the Critical Voice exercise (see Chapter 7), he became very familiar with the harsh voice with which he spoke to himself. He recognized that voice didn't necessarily have a valid viewpoint. Before a meeting with new people, he began to imagine sending his Critical Voice away to the mountains all by itself. We also practiced asking open-ended questions and summarizing what he heard as two ways to contribute to the conversation even without forming an independent opinion.

The more Raj spoke up, the more it created a virtuous cycle; one success built upon the last. Soon, he found himself more engaged in conversations and adding his expertise, even when new people were in the meetings. Several clients commented on the value he was adding to solve their problems. With each success in speaking up, he became less nervous about doing it again. He realized he had an important viewpoint, particularly with his background in privacy, which others did not have. He reported that he was proud he recognized what was preventing him from speaking up and was continuing to focus on his strengths so that he could challenge himself in other ways. Raj's mantra was "Say it!"

Insignificance to Impact: Patricia's Story

Patricia, a product manager in a large tech company, felt like her skills and experiences were not getting her the progress she wanted. She was feeling self-doubt, had trouble speaking up in meetings, stumbled in presentations, and felt like she was not making the impact she wanted. And she was stressed out, with a young son at home with whom she never felt very present after a long day. Despite her strong work ethic and volume of deliverables, she felt invisible.

After visualizing her Wisdom Within to build her confidence and experimenting with ways to speak up and present her ideas, Patricia began actively asking more questions in meetings, even when she had not yet fully formed her ideas. She scheduled one-on-ones with key engineering partners she had to influence to build a relationship and get their perspectives. She gave herself grace when she did not do something perfect, which allowed her to show up as her more authentic self. That self-empathy gave her more courage to share ideas and not hold back.

Soon she was more comfortable sharing her ideas, even when a meeting was larger and included colleagues or executives she didn't know well. Her engineering partners started inviting her to meetings and asking for her advice. She was able to influence her leadership to include one of her ideas into the next product build.

Previously, Patricia had felt no one listened to her. Gradually, she started seeing that she was having a visible impact. She realized the company and the customers were better off because she was able to share her ideas, influence others, and have impact. Her presentations became smoother. She stumbled less, especially when she visualized her Wisdom Within before a presentation.

She continued to experiment with speaking up and showing up more confidently. She got praise from her boss on her improved performance, even though her work output did not change. Her behaviors and her mindset had changed. And her young son appreciated that mommy was not so stressed when she came home from work and was willing to play Legos. Patricia told herself to "say it and show up."

Asking for a Promotion: Jessica's Story

As a senior finance manager at a financial services company, Jessica was used to putting her head down, doing great work, and being recognized by her supportive leaders. But once she got one leadership level shy of what her company called the director level, she felt stagnant. Her boss praised her deliverables but would never mention anything about a potential promotion. True to her introvert tendencies, her strong Critical Voice told her that she was not good enough to be promoted. She also observed how outgoing all the directors were. With her quiet nature, she felt that she could never be like them and was too reticent to ask for the promotion, in case her boss did not think she was ready.

Still, Jessica eventually realized that what had gotten her to her current leadership level was not going to get her to the next level. Working together, she became aware of her Critical Voice and realized she had a choice in the way she thought. She decided to reduce her negative self-talk by sending her Critical Voice to the Bahamas, which helped her become calmer and more confident.

Though she wanted to get promoted, she was hesitant and nervous about becoming the "big boss." She was worried that the other directors would not respect her quiet style and a potential new team would not follow her direction. After lots of reflection, she realized she could not wait for external validation from her boss or colleagues that she was ready; she had to act.

That's when Jessica began trying out things that were uncomfortable, like making sure she shared an idea or question in every meeting. To become more comfortable being the center of attention in a meeting, she connected to her purpose in being there, which was to share an idea, not to hog the spotlight. She talked with others who'd made the jump to director and made an assessment of her own strengths of analytical and strategic thinking, collaboration, and ability to get things done.

When she felt ready, she spoke with her boss about an open director role on his team. He welcomed the discussion. He did not think she wanted to get promoted, as she had never talked about her aspiration. As she went through the interviews for the director position, Jessica got more confident. She knew she had the subject-matter expertise and also knew she could develop the skills to lead and manage people despite her style differences with her potential new colleagues. In fact, many of them commented that her quiet, analytical style would be an asset to the team dynamic.

Jessica got the job!

Of course, her Critical Voice tried to sneak back in, telling her she was not worthy, but she had the tools to send it to the beach and focus on her purpose of impacting the business at a higher level and developing her team. She used all the tools and insights from coaching as she onboarded to her new, higher role.

One specific goal she had was to show up as her authentic introverted self, not as a mimic of her extroverted colleagues. We discussed all the ways she could add value that were not about being the loudest in staff meetings, such as meeting in smaller groups, sending memos, and connecting to key influencers. With continued practice and time in the job, the self-doubt melted away and she felt at peace. That calmness enabled her to have the clarity of thinking to develop her team's strategy.

Her professional progress would have never happened if she had not quieted her Critical Voice and gotten out of her comfort zone to ask for a promotion. Her subsequent success as a new director came from experimenting with new behaviors of sharing her perspective and authentic behaviors as an introverted leader—observation, curiosity, reflection, analysis, follow-up. She could harness her own strengths and did not need to show up as an extrovert. It was natural. She became the confident leader that she had dreamed of because she spoke up and showed up.

Embracing Confident Leadership: Michael's Story

After a company he started was bought out by a larger biomedical company, Michael struggled to feel confident in his new vice president position. While he'd had no problem making decisions and directing his team while leading his own company, once he was part of a larger organization, he had trouble standing up for his ideas in the new culture. He had trouble understanding the political dynamics of the organization. His reserved nature did not fit into the more boisterous corporate culture. He felt like his colleagues focused on strutting around like roosters in leadership meetings while he would quietly focus on leading his team in developing new innovations.

Michael's boss in the biomedical company said Michael was not going to be successful unless he learned a way to gain the respect of his more extroverted colleagues. At first, Michael tried to be more outspoken in meetings, but he felt he had to interrupt people and it was exhausting. He felt he was not his authentic self.

Through our discussions, Michael realized he was trying to use a style that he thought his boss and colleagues wanted him to use but did not come naturally to him. The light bulb went off that he was never going to be them, so he decided to focus on his strengths: innovative thinking, team development, and observation. He let go of seeking external validation and focused on doing what he thought was right. He worried a little about his colleagues judging him harshly, but he just let it go. If they pushed back on one of his ideas, he saw it as a gift, giving him insights on how to make the product better.

Yes, he did have to speak up more in meetings. But he would also complement that by coming back one-on-one with a colleague to influence them on an idea that perhaps he hadn't had enough airtime in the meeting to sell. Originally, he was hesitant to send emails to his bosses and colleagues unless he was fully confident he had thought through all the details. He challenged himself to start sending emails describing unperfected, newly formed ideas to his boss and colleagues, which allowed him to get their input and buy-in before the ideas were finished.

Gradually, Michael went from stressed, depleted, and not feeling like he fit in to confident, energized, relaxed, and happier. And his team appreciated the relationships he was building with his colleagues. They trusted that he could get the resources and collaboration from partner teams with his growing influence in the corporation. And just as importantly, he had the courage and confidence to trust himself.

Not only did Michael's team produce more innovative products in the next year, but he was getting more sleep and had made time for exercising. He had never felt better. His business was more visible, and he was showing up in the forums he had not been included in before. His CEO started bringing him to board meetings where he had to remind himself of all the insights he'd used when he first joined the corporation: trust himself and be his authentic introverted self. When he was able to "say it, send it, show up," he had a much greater impact on the business and his life.

It's Deliberate Work, Not Magic

I have been lucky to observe the transformation of all my clients to becoming more confident, impactful leaders. One even said I used magic. But really, they did all the work, using the tools and insights captured in this book. You, too, can experience this transformation if you choose to. It is a lifelong practice to use your strengths as an introvert and experiment with your behaviors to be even more impactful. Change behaviors, not who you are.

It starts with confidence in believing you have value to add to the world. And you do—you just have to let it out. People I have coached are still their introverted selves; they are just better at speaking up, influencing, and connecting with other people. They are more satisfied and proud of the changes in their behavior and mindset and the impact of their leadership and careers. And it has spilled into their personal lives. They are happier and less stressed. Their loved ones see the changes. Again, they are still who they are, just better. Join us to lead with quiet confidence.

CHANGE BEHAVIORS, NOT WHO YOU ARE.

14

Setting Your Own Direction

Introverts, the world needs you and it needs
the things you carry. So I wish you the best of all
possible journeys and the courage to speak softly.
—Susan Cain

Shonda Rhimes, a highly successful writer and producer of TV shows such as *Gray's Anatomy* and *Scandal* and a self-proclaimed introvert, always declined invitations to speak or attend events. As a new trustee of the Kennedy Center, she was invited to sit in the presidential box of the Kennedy Center with President Obama and the First Lady. She realized if she had been *asked*, she would have said no, but she'd been *told* to sit there. In her book, *Year of Yes*, she states:

"I would have said no because if I had said yes, I would have had to actually do it. I would have had to actually go and sit in the box and be there to meet the President and the First Lady. I would have had to make small talk and say things. I would have had to drink cocktails near

Carlos Santana. I would have had to do all the things that I, in fact, *did do* that night. And I had a wonderful time. When all was said and done, it was one of the most memorable nights of my life."

Her book is about reflecting on all the things she had missed out on from saying no and trying a new behavior: saying yes. As you can imagine, she expanded her world, but she also remained the same quiet person who liked to think and create new story ideas in solitude. She changed behaviors, not who she was.

Ms. Rhimes can serve as an inspiration to all of us introverts. Throughout this book, I've shared ideas about how to be successful and confident as an introvert without changing who you are. I've focused on changing a mindset or a behavior while embracing your strengths. You do not have to be an extrovert to succeed. You can make the changes you want to make to be more impactful in your job, in your life. In this chapter, I want to give you more advice on launching a successful journey to quiet leadership.

Identify Your Internal Resources

I don't know any adult who thinks behavior change is easy. It requires persistent action, courage, and conscious thought to effectively change how we interact with the world. Identifying your internal resources will help you maintain the focus and energy you'll need to succeed on this path. Here, I'll focus on three of them: your passions, your values, and your strengths.

Your Passions Will Give You Conviction

Introverts can have challenges with speaking up. As we saw with Gandhi, if you are connected with your passion, you can more easily speak up.

You can also use your passion and values as ways to reframe doing things you may not want to do, such as speaking up or networking.

Think of a time you overcame your preference to stay quiet and instead spoke up. What was this experience where you were living your values and passionate about what you wanted to say and spoke up despite any qualms or discomforts you may have had? Perhaps the topic was something you truly believed in or you were standing up for someone else, such as your child, a best friend, or your team. Maybe you felt comfortable with the people you were speaking to, had practiced speaking up beforehand, or had a previous success in doing this. Whatever the reason, take time to remember the time you spoke up and build on that experience and what you learned.

For me, it was an experience in my previous career when we were discussing the launch date of a new product with the leadership team. The date selected was Rosh Hashanah, one of the holiest days in Judaism. No one thought it was a big deal, and only one other person on the leadership team besides me was Jewish. Together, we spoke up and explained this was the equivalent of launching a product on Christmas Eve. They got it. They still decided to launch on that day but changed the date in Israel.

This solution was not my preference, but I was glad I had at least spoken up and influenced a change. In some ways, this situation was no different from others I had encountered in my career: I knew I had knowledge most others did not. I also had the support of colleagues. What pushed me over the edge this time and gave me the courage to speak up was my passion for doing the right thing for our customers. All these factors drove me to get past my discomfort to disagree with the rest of the team and speak up to drive a change.

What things are you passionate about or have little problem talking about to others? What is it you talk about and if you get started, it is hard for you to stop? What do you love to do? What problem are you longing to address in the world? Maybe it is gardening or rock climbing or doing puzzles or teaching children or rescuing animals.

I am passionate about helping leaders develop. I love helping my team develop their individual leadership skills. And then when I started coaching, I realized I was passionate about helping introverts find their voice. When I talk to anyone about this passion, no one believes I am an introvert, as I can't stop talking.

If you can't identify your passion at first, that is OK. Think of a list of things that could be contenders, that you strongly like but perhaps would not call "passions." Start paying attention both in and out of work about what's going on when you get the courage to speak up, and use that to help identify a passion that will give you the courage, confidence, and conviction to change.

Your Values

According to *Psychology Today*, "Core values serve as guiding principles that shape our attitudes, actions, and decisions. According to psychological research, values are fundamental beliefs that guide our choices and behaviors."

You can search online for a list of values and pick your top five or refer to the References section for a website that will rank your values. If you have already identified your values elsewhere, use that list. If you want to add attributes not listed, go ahead. Either way, note your top five values on a piece of paper or in the workbook.

As I discussed in Chapter 5, identifying my values helped provide clarity for me on my change in career path, becoming a leadership coach. *Development* and *awe* were newly added to my top five values, replacing *achievement* and *respect*. This change in values also helped me realize what topics I love talking about. So in conversations with new people, I love to guide the conversation to what they are learning or an awe-inspiring experience or vacation they had recently.

I had one client who identified one value: *gratitude*. She went through her day, at work and home, making sure she was living and breathing gratitude. When she was upset with the way a project was going, she would think about what she was grateful for, such as the learning opportunity or the relationships she'd built. When her kids were whining when they were tired at the end of the day, she would think of her gratitude for the loving family she had. She intentionally lived her value.

Knowing your values can also counteract your Critical Voice, helping you recognize what you *don't* value (such as others' judgment of you). In that way, reconnecting with your values allows you to let things go. In short, identifying your values can help guide your decisions and also the way you want to be in the world, where you want to spend your time, and what you care about in others.

Your Strengths

Scott Barry Kaufman, author of *Transcend*, states, "In trying to figure out the deeper aspects of yourself that are the best within you (i.e., your best selves), it might be helpful to assess your 'signature strength,' or the particular aspects of your personality that you yearn to use, that enable authentic expression, and that energize you and give you a sense of vitality. These include your various talents and your character strength—those aspects of your personality that specifically contribute to the good life for yourself and for others."

Naturally, you are going to be more confident when you can draw on traits you think of as strengths. Think about what your strengths are.

Are they some of the ones we mentioned—thoughtful, focused, good listener—that are superpowers of introverts? What else are you strong in?

These could be leadership attributes, but I would consider looking more broadly into your personal life as well.

What feedback do you consistently get from others about areas where you perform well? For example, do you find the win-win solution? Are you direct and don't get tied up with emotions? Do you excel at research to find the best answer? Think of a time you performed really well. What were you doing? What skills or knowledge were you using?

Defining Your Own Path to Action

Perhaps you have already begun experimenting with the action ideas presented in previous chapters. If so, then use this last section to help you confirm your course of action and pick the next things to work on. If you have not already experimented, pick one thing in the book you want to try.

Either way, I urge you to build on the foundation of your passions, goals, and strengths to help shape an action path tailored to you. Here are three steps to get you started.

Don't forget to download the *Lead with Quiet Confidence Workbook* to work through the exercises in this book at www.JenniferMarcou.com/resources or scan the QR code below.

1. Identify Your Goals

In addition to talking about strengths, Kaufman goes on to cite research that found the content of one's strivings also matters. Kennon Sheldon, a graduate student of Robert Emmoms (a leader in the positive psychology movement), states, "Goals that are conducive to growth—mastery, self-improvement, creativity, connection, contribution to society—are likely to lead to greater well-being than goals concerned with status and driven by insecurity—attaining power, money, self-esteem, appearance, or popularity."

If your goals are concordant or aligned with your own growth versus externally driven goals, it will enable you to put more effort into achieving those goals. Kaufman states, "A large body of research suggests that choosing self-concordant goals has important implications not only for setting off an upward spiral of growth, fulfillment, and well-being but also for the amount of effort you are willing to put into the striving—and the likelihood that you will eventually *attain* the goal." Clear goals that relate to your growth allow you to be more focused and let go of the unimportant (like negative self-rumination) and enable you to be more successful at achieving those goals—positive reinforcement to do more.

Let's revisit your reflections from Chapter 3. What were the reasons you picked up this book in the first place? Were there particular behaviors you wanted to get better at? Were there uncomfortable feelings about being an introvert that you wanted to change? Reflect on what your original intentions were for taking the time to read this book and identify what your intentions are now. Now identify your overall goals in the changes you want to make in your leadership. What do you want to work on to have more impact, build your confidence, and be your authentic self as a leader? What would bring you more happiness at work? Write down your goals in the workbook or in your own notes.

Goal #1 ______________________________

Goal #2 ______________________________

Goal #3 ______________________________

2. Define Your Comfort Zones

This next step is designed to help you match your goals with areas of comfort and discomfort. You will determine behaviors or skills you are comfortable with and where your growing edge is—where you can push the boundaries of your comfort zone out just a little bit.

Start by picking one goal and filling in the graphic in Figure 14.1. What do you already do now that is related to that goal (Zone 1)? What could you do that would be slightly uncomfortable (Zone 2)? What would your ideal end goal be—something you find extremely uncomfortable now but exemplifies your goal (Zone 3)?

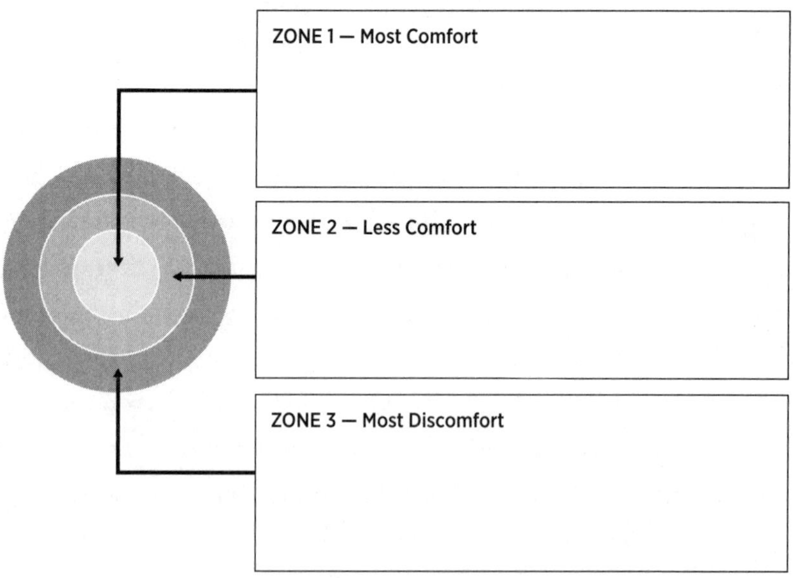

Figure 14.1: Your comfort zones

REMEMBER TO BE KIND

As we explored in Chapter 3, one key to success in creating behavioral change is to set Kind goals: an incremental change you can make that won't be too stressful but will move you in the direction you want. Kind goals are something that are easy to do or experiment with.

3. Define How You Will Experiment with That Change (LEAD with Quiet Confidence Framework)

Once you have written down all your ideas in Zones 1, 2, and 3, circle *one thing* in Zone 2 or 3 that you want to work toward. Next, you'll want to do one thing out of your comfort zone at work.

DO ONE THING OUT OF YOUR COMFORT ZONE AT WORK.

Use the LEAD with Quiet Confidence Framework to help you identify what change you will experiment with.

- L—What is the learning objective?
- E—What is the experiment you want to try? Make it Kind.
- A—How did you assess yourself? How did it go? What did you learn? How did you celebrate taking the action?
- D—What do you want to incorporate into your development plan? What will you continue doing, start or stop doing, or modify? What do you want to try next? (Repeat the LEAD with Quiet Confidence Framework.)

For example, if your goal is to speak up in more meetings, instead of stating that you will speak up five times in every meeting (which would take you straight to Zone 3), you could identify the Kind goal of speaking up in one meeting once a day. You experiment with that action for a week, then assess the results. If speaking up was easier and you got positive reactions, then you can expand the goal. Or perhaps you learn that you fumbled verbally too much when speaking so you decide to do more preparation and write down bullet points before each meeting.

DRAW ON YOUR INNER COMPASS

As you work to define your own path, remember to draw on your Inner Compass, as discussed in Chapters 5 and 6. Be more mindful as you go through your days. Learn to listen to your intuition. Focus on your purpose. Be compassionate with yourself. And above all, learn how to hear the voice of your Wisdom Within, which represents your future best self, your intuition, and your purpose combined. This voice already exists inside of you. But sometimes it is very quiet, and it is hard to hear over all the other Critical Voices and busyness of life. So the best way to connect with your future self is to pause, breathe, and reconnect.

Your Life, Your Path

As I said in the Introduction, I wrote this book to help introverts learn ideas and techniques that took me years of experience to learn. I want to accelerate your learning. But the benefit of this book is not to be received just by reading it—it is by taking action. It is you experimenting with the concepts and starting with Kind goals. It is doing one thing out of your comfort zone. It is "saying it, sending it, showing up." It is you finding the path that works for you. I don't want to turn you into a cookie-cutter, successful introvert. Change your behaviors, not who you are. I want you to blossom into the creative, resourceful, confident, successful, and unique person you already are. I want you to be proud of your introversion. But mostly, I want you to be proud of yourself. Step into yourself and lead with quiet confidence.

Epilogue

My Hope for You

The privilege of a lifetime is to
become who you really are.
—Carl Jung

Remember the story I told at the very beginning of this book? I broke down in tears during a training session when I recognized myself in the story of a woman not being heard, remembering all the times I had felt exactly that way. I now visualize that the woman in the scenario has read this book and tried one or two of the tools. When the man reiterates her idea without giving credit, I imagine her saying, "What a great idea I said a few minutes ago."

OK, that is a little snarky, but I reclaim the experience for myself, for her, and for all introverts. *You* have great ideas. *You* have an impact on the world. And you can have even more impact and still be authentic to your brain, personality, and temperament. It is your choice to make.

Above all else, I hope you take away from this book a sense of pride in being an introvert. Introverts are amazing! We are innovators and writers and business leaders and cultural icons and peacekeepers. Introversion is not something we should feel embarrassed about or something to be cured; it is something we were born with, which provides us with superpowers. The world would not have the scientific findings of Marie Curie, Albert Einstein, and Nikola Tesla without introverts. We would not have ubiquitous computers or social connections online without fellow introverts Bill Gates, Steve Wozniak, and Mark Zuckerberg. We would not have the beautiful words, insights, and entertainment from Emily Dickinson, Agatha Christie, and J. K. Rowling—all introverts. We would not have people who broke barriers and set the tone of our culture without introverted Oprah Winfrey, Shonda Rhimes, and Rosa Parks. We would not have the creativity of inward-seeking Steven Spielberg, Meryl Streep, and Elton John. We would not have peace at key times without the powerful introverts Mahatma Gandhi, Abraham Lincoln, and Nelson Mandela.

Introverts are thoughtful, empathetic, creative, great listeners, and great leaders. And you are one of them! Use your superpowers to make the impact you want to have.

WORKING WITH THE AUTHOR

Beyond that belief in yourself, I hope you have found value in this book and have some takeaways that can lead you to greater success in whatever career path you want to take, whether it's having more confidence and influence in your current job or moving up the hierarchy.

I have used many of the concepts and tools in this book in my coaching and training programs. Hundreds of my clients have become more successful by using these tools. I know they can help you if you try them. If you want more personalized help in identifying solutions specific to you or want more guidance in the implementation and sustainability of the changes you have made, reach out for potential coaching or training. I can be reached at www.JenniferMarcou.com.

I am also available for keynote speeches or workshops on introverted leadership in your company, conferences, or associations. Please don't hesitate to reach out to me at www.JenniferMarcou.com.

Acknowledgments

This book would never have happened without a long list of people to support, teach, mentor, and inspire me. As an introvert, I thought writing a book would be a solo project—me alone in my thoughts and writing. The book literally flowed out of my head, but I realize how much was shaped by others who have taught and inspired me. The reality is the book never would have seen the light of day without many, many people.

First, I would like to thank my two editors, Erin Gordon and Sue Reynard, without whom the book would not be half as good as it is. Erin Gordon first inspired me to move from dreaming about writing a book to believing I could do it. And then she helped me become a better writer by editing my first draft. She helped me tell a better story. Sue Reynard from Greenleaf Publishing put the music to the manuscript. I had written a song, and she rearranged it and added violins and vocals to make it sing (in addition to making it clearer, more succinct, and more impactful).

Second, I would like to thank the coaches who supported and encouraged me along the way. The insightful coaches I worked with on developing the Lead with Quiet Confidence program were all critical to developing several of the frameworks and organization of the material. Thank you, Janet Williams Hepler, Noam King, Dan Stahl, and April McCormick. All the hours you put in together to design, then deliver the programs were a great testing ground. We proved that we can help introverts lead without changing who they are. Thank you, Patty Burgin, for your inspirational coaching training at SeattleCoach and for creating forums where these amazing coaches can come together with a passion to help introverts. It all started with you. And if I go back a little further, I have to thank Rosie Mastrandrea for introducing me to coaching and to Patty. You forever changed the direction of my life to follow my passion for coaching.

Thank you to the M5 group of coaches, Paula Boos, Cathy Moore, Jennifer Winick, and Julia Atalla, who supported me on a weekly basis in the ups and downs of writing the book. Thank you to Annie Ricci for providing opportunities to hone my craft with hundreds of clients she generously shared. And a shout-out to her amazing group of coaches who were there in spirit. Thank you to Jill Thiry from Rancho La Puerta for the idea of Kind goals. Thank you Matt Rudnitsky of Platypus Publishing whose class gave me the structure and scaffolding for starting my book. Thank you to Robert Jones, my boss at American Express, for introducing me to the ABCDEs of Influence.

Third, I want to thank my beta readers who were willing to read through the second version of the manuscript and provide me insights to make this the best book it could be. Thank you, Courtney Keppler, Holly Harrison, Mark Meadows, Naeemah Ruffin, Lisa Vergara, Emi Ristani, Dan Stahl, and Noam King. And a special thanks to John Medina for providing feedback on the brain science chapter.

I want to thank Greenleaf Publishing. Thank you, Dee Kerr, who took a chance on a first-time author. You saw the potential for what this book could be. Thank you, Maxine Marshall, Benito Salazar, Hannah Marlow, Hayden Seder, Brittany Jones-Pugh, Rachel High,

Matt Baganz, and the many others who supported my publishing journey.

Thank you to those who helped with the marketing. Brand Builders Group was heaven-sent to me by Shannon Huffman Polson. Thank you, Rory and AJ Vaden, for your brilliance and sharing it in such a compelling way with the community. Thank you to my BBG coach Melinda Hinson, who supported me at every step. Thank you, Isla Lake at Mission Driven Press, for fulfillment. Thank you, Becky Robinson and Wendy Haan of Weaving Influence, for all the insights and work on marketing the book.

Thank you to all the authors who were so generous with their time and insights. Whether it was how to self-publish or hybrid-publish or how to get a testimonial, your insights were invaluable. Thank you to all the coaches and authors who inspired me in my coaching and many ideas in my book, particularly Shirzad Chamine, Tara Mohr, and Susan Cain.

Thank you to my clients and participants in the Lead with Quiet Confidence programs. You have inspired me with your willingness to learn and evolve. Thank you for letting me be part of your journey.

Thank you to The Chapin School and specifically Mrs. Putnam and Mrs. Rinden for teaching this science and math geek how to write. While I did not find the joy of writing in high school, I do now realize how lucky I was for your teachings to enable me to be successful in business and in writing a book. Who knew?

I would be remiss if I did not thank my family. I thank my parents, Susan Singer and John Hudson, for pushing me out of my comfort zone, whether it was trying a new food, traveling to a new place, or making those dreaded calls to order pizza. You instilled in me the belief I can do things that are hard, or things I don't like, to build my confidence. Thank you to my stepparents, Anita Colombo and Paul Singer, for your support and backing in my formative years to build my independence.

Thank you to my kids, Nikita, Nadia, and Damon, who inspired me to share my thoughts to help other introverts leverage their strengths sooner than it took me. And last but not least, thank you to my husband, Rick, who had the patience to read through the very first draft, had the willingness to discuss all my ponderings, and encouraged me at every stage. You inspired humor in the book and throughout the process. Thank you—I love you!

References

Introduction: Join the Quiet Awakening of Introverts

"When introverts fully embrace who we are . . ."

- Michaela Chung, *The Irresistible Introvert: Harness the Power of Quiet Charisma in a Loud World* (Simon and Schuster, 2016).

Chapter 1: Introversion and Quiet Confidence

Myers-Briggs definition of introversion

- Kevin Wood, "Introversion 2.0: What We Need to Reshape the Way We Work," Myers-Briggs, December 28, 2021, https://www.themyersbriggs.com/en-US/Access-Resources/Articles/introversion-2-why-we-need-to-reshape-the-way-we-work.

Definition of introversion

- Susan Cain, *Quiet: The Power of Introverts in a World That Can't Stop Talking* (Crown Publishing Group, 2013).

Introversion as a temperament

- Jenn Granneman, *The Secret Lives of Introverts: Inside Our Hidden World (Simon and Sc*huster, 2017).

Difference between shyness and introversion

- Susan Cain, "Shyness and Introversion Are Not the Same Thing," *Psychology Today*, July 6, 2011, https://www.psychologytoday.com/us/blog/quiet-the-power-introverts/201107/are-you-shy-introverted-both-or-neither-and-why-does-it?msockid=06e22881e6fe606838173c37e744619e.

HEXACO Personality Inventory

- "The HEXACO Personality Inventory - Revised," HEXACO, https://hexaco.org/hexaco-online.

Are extroverts happier?

- Peter Hills and Michael Argyle, "Happiness, Introversion—Extraversion and Happy Introverts," *Personality and Individual Differences* 30, no. 4 (March 1, 2001): 595–608, https://doi.org/10.1016/s0191-8869(00)00058-1.

Challenges of being an introverted leader

- Jennifer Kahnweiler, *The Introverted Leader: Building on your Quiet Strength*, 2nd ed. (Barrett-Koehler Publishers, 2018).

What is a leader?

- Young Entrepreneur Council (YEC), "Six Ways to Lead Even When You Aren't in a Leadership Position," *Forbes*, May 3, 2023, https://www.forbes.com/councils/theyec/2023/05/03/six-ways-to-lead-even-when-you-arent-in-a-leadership-position/.

Executive leaders score higher in extroversion in the Big Five Assessment than any other leadership lower level.

- Deniz S. Ones and Stephan Dilchert, "How Special Are Executives? How Special Should Executive Selection Be? Observations and Recommendations," *Industrial and Organizational Psychology* 2, no. 2 (May 29, 2009): 163–70, https://doi.org/10.1111/j.1754-9434.2009.01127.x.
- Elizabeth Bernstein, "Why Introverts Make Great Entrepreneurs," *The Wall Street Journal*, August 24, 2015, https://www.wsj.com/articles/why-introverts-make-great-entrepreneurs-1440381699.

"65 percent of senior executives see introversion as a 'barrier to leadership,' and only 6 percent think introverts have the people skills required to oversee a successful team."

- Zachary Crockett, "Why Introverts Make Great Leaders," *The Hustle*, July 14, 2018, https://thehustle.co/why-introverts-make-great-leaders.

Quotes from famous introverts

- "55 Most Famous Introverts Who Changed the World," Science of People, November 25, 2025, https://www.scienceofpeople.com/famous-introverts/.

Quote from Eleanor Roosevelt

- Eleanor Roosevelt, "My Day, January 1, 1936," The Eleanor Roosevelt Papers Digital Edition, 2017, https://www2.gwu.edu/~erpapers/myday/displaydocedits.cfm?_y=1936&_f=md054221a.

Strengths of introverted leaders

- Aguimar Neto, "Why Introverts Excel as Leaders: 7 Key Traits That Set Them Apart," *The Introvert Blog*, November 20, 2023, https://theintrovertblog.com/why-introverts-make-good-leaders/.
- Gladys Kong, "Embracing Unique Strengths: Why Introverts Make Great Leaders," *Forbes*, June 26, 2023, https://www.forbes.com/councils/forbestechcouncil/2023/06/26/embracing-unique-strengths-why-introverts-make-great-leaders/.
- Benjamin Laker, "The Quiet, Transformative Power of Introverted Leaders," *Forbes*, October 14, 2024, https://www.forbes.com/sites/benjaminlaker/2024/10/14/the-quiet-transformative-power-of-introverted-leaders/.

Introverts are better leaders of proactive teams.

- Adam Grant, Francesca Gino, and David Hoffman, "The Hidden Advantages of Quiet Bosses," *Harvard Business Review*, December 1, 2010, https://hbr.org/2010/12/the-hidden-advantages-of-quiet-bosses.

Story of Mahatma Gandhi

- Cain, *Quiet*.

Chapter 2: Appreciating the Brilliance of Your Introvert Brain

Differences in the introverted brain

- Peter Hollins, *The Science of Introverts: Explore the Personality Spectrum for Self-Discovery, Self-Awareness, & Self-Care*. Design a Life That Fits (Publish Drive, 2024).

Introverts have more gray and white matter.

- Lea J. Forsman, Örjan de Manzano, Anke Karabanov, Guy Madison, and Fredrik Ullén, "Differences in Regional Brain Volume Related to the Extraversion–Introversion Dimension—A Voxel Based Morphometry Study," *Neuroscience Research* 72, no. 1 (October 17, 2011): 59–67, https://doi.org/10.1016/j.neures.2011.10.001.

"takes us longer to verbalize our thoughts is that introverts rely on long-term memory . . ."

- Chung, *The Irresistible Introvert.*

Introverts use a different pathway in their brains.

- Debra L. Johnson, John S. Wiebe, Sherri M. Gold et al., "Cerebral Blood Flow and Personality: A Positron Emission Tomography Study," *American Journal of Psychiatry* 156, no. 2 (February 1, 1999): 252–57, https://doi.org/10.1176/ajp.156.2.252.
- Michelle Gallagher, "The Difference Between Introverts and Extroverts," *Psychology Today*, July 1, 1999, https://www.psychologytoday.com/us/articles/199907/the-difference
-between-introverts-and-extroverts?msockid=06e22881e6fe-606838173c37e744619e.
- Holley Gerth, The Powerful Purpose of Introverts: Why the World Needs You to Be You (Revell, 2020).
- Holley Gerth, "Being an Introvert Isn't the Same as Social Distancing," *Holley Gerth*, June 24, 2020, https://holleygerth.com/being-an-introvert-isnt-the-same-as-social-distancing/#:~:text=When%20Dr.%20Debra%20Johnson%20scanned%20the%20brains%20of,pathway%20is%20longer%2C%20more%20complex%2C%20and%20internally%20focused.

Introverts take longer to take action.

- Michael Houlihan and Robert M. Stelmack, "Extraversion and Motor Response Initiation," *Journal of Individual Differences* 32, no. 2 (January 1, 2011): 103–9, https://doi.org/10.1027/1614-0001/a000041.

Introverts have more blood flow in the frontal cortex.

- Johnson et al., "Cerebral Blood Flow."

Understanding of how dopamine operates in introverted versus extroverted brains

- Marti Olsen Laney, *The Introvert Advantage: How Quiet People Can Thrive in an Extrovert World* (Workman Publishing Company, 2002).

Introverts have a higher level of activation in their brains.

- H. J. Eysenck, "Biological Basis of Personality," *Nature* 199, no. 4898 (September 1, 1963): 1031–34, https://doi.org/10.1038/1991031a0.
- H. J. Eysenck, *The Biological Basis of Personality* (Thomas, 1967).

Introverts create more saliva with lemon juice on the tongue.

- Kevin Bennett, "The Lemon Test: Introverts Are More Aroused Than Extroverts," *Psychology Today*, August 31, 2021, https://www.psychologytoday.com/us/blog/modern-minds/202108/the-lemon-test-introverts-are-more-aroused-extroverts?msoc-kid=06e22881e6fe606838173c37e744619e.

Introverts have higher glutamate in dorsolateral prefrontal cortex and negatively associated with state anxiety.

- Simone Grimm, Florian Schubert, Maren Jaedke, Jürgen Gallinat, and Malek Bajbouj, "Prefrontal Cortex Glutamate and Extraversion," *Social Cognitive and Affective Neuroscience* 7, no. 7 (October 20, 2011): 811–18, https://doi.org/10.1093/scan/nsr056.

Introverts are more rewarded by acetylcholine and parasympathetic nervous system.

- Laney, The I*ntrovert Advantage*.
- Christine Fonseca, *Quiet Kids: Help Your Introverted Child Succeed in an Extroverted World* (Routledge, 2021).

Chapter 3: Leading the Changes You Want to Make

"Introversion does not change. But our behaviors can change . . ."

- Gerth, The *Powerful Purpose of Introverts*.

Make it easy.

- James Clear, *Atomic Habits* (Random House Business Books, 2018).

Micro habits

- Sabina Nawaz, *You're the Boss: Become the Manager You Want to Be (and Others Need)* (Simon and Schuster, 2025).

Tiny habits

- B. J. Fogg, *Tiny Habits: The Small Changes That Change Everything* (Harvest, 2020).

Fear of talking to strangers

- David Robson, "Awkward? The Science of How to Make People Like You," *The Times*, June 2, 2024, https://www.thetimes.com/life-style/health-fitness/article/science-how-make-people-like-you-david-robson-advice-k2vxgr2z6?utm_source=chatgpt.com®ion=global.

"Thinking is for doing" and mirror neurons to modify other people's brains

- Richard M. Restak, *The Naked Brain: How the Emerging Neurosociety Is Changing How We Live, Work, and Love* (Harmony, 2006).

Frameworks for change

- Mel Robbins and Sawyer Robbins, *The Let Them Theory: A Life-Changing Tool That Millions of People Can't Stop Talking About* (Hay House, Inc, 2024).
- Shirzad Chamine, *Positive Intelligence: Why Only 20% of Teams and Individuals Achieve Their True Potential and How You Can Achieve Yours* (Greenleaf Book Group, 2012).
- Tara Mohr, *Playing Big: Find Your Voice, Your Mission, Your Message* (Penguin, 2014).
- Jill Bolte Taylor, Whole Brain Living: The Anatomy of Choice and the Four Charact*ers That Drive Our Life* (Hay House, Inc, 2021).

How celebrating connects to motivation

- Melanie A. McNally, "From Small Steps to Big Wins: The Importance of Celebrating," *Psychology Today*, June 12, 2024, https://www.psychologytoday.com/us/blog/empower-your-mind/202406/from-small-steps-to-big-wins-the-importance-of-celebrating#:~:text=Celebrating%20wins%20activates%20the%20brain%27s%20reward%20system%2C%20boosting,helps%20solidify%20lessons%20learned%2C%20fostering%20intentional%20future%20actions.?msockid=06e22881e6fe606838173c37e744619e.

Chapter 4: Competence, Meet Confidence

"The most important attitude we have may be the attitude we have toward ourselves . . ."

- Scott Barry Kaufman, *Transcend: The New Science of Self-Actualization and How It Can Transform Your Life* (Tarcher, 2020).

Confidence is more important than competence.

- Cameron Anderson, Sebastien Brion, Don Moore, and Jessica Kennedy, "A Status-Enhancement Account of Overconfidence," *Journal of Personality and Social Psychology* 103, no. 4 (January 1, 2012): 718–35, https://doi.org/10.1037/a0029395.

Confidence wins . . .

- Kaufman, Transcend.
- Roy F. Baumeister, Jennifer D. Campbell, Joachim I. Krueger, and Kathleen D. Vohs, "Does High Self-Esteem Cause Better Performance, Interpersonal Success, Happiness, or Healthier Lifestyles?," *Psychological Science in the Public Interest* 4, no. 1 (May 1, 2003): 1–44, https://doi.org/10.1111/1529-1006.01431.
- Ed Diener and Marissa Diener, "Cross-Cultural Correlates of Life Satisfaction and Self-Esteem," *Journal of Personality and Social Psychology* 68, no. 4 (January 1, 1995): 653–63, https://doi.org/10.1037/0022-3514.68.4.653.
- Ulrich Orth, Richard Robins, Kali Trzesniewski, Jürgen Maes, and Manfred Schmitt, "Low Self-Esteem Is a Risk Factor for Depressive Symptoms from Young Adulthood to Old Age," *Journal of Abnormal Psychology* 118, no. 3 (August 1, 2009): 472–78, https://doi.org/10.1037/a0015922.

"Success correlates more closely with confidence than it does with competence." "Failure is a critical partner of confidence . . ."

- Katty Kay and Claire Shipman, *The Confidence Code: The Science and Art of* Self-*Assurance—What Women Should Know* (HarperBusiness, 2015).

"The more successful you are at making progress toward your goals, the more confident you feel . . ."

- Kaufman, *Transcend.*

Caroline Miller quote: "Confidence comes from stepping out of your comfort zone . . ."

- Kay and Shipman, The *Confidence Code.*

Women underestimate their abilities more than men.

- Joyce Ehrlinger and David Dunning, "How Chronic Self-Views Influence (and Potentially Mislead) Estimates of Performance," *Journal of Personality and Social Psychology* 84, no. 1 (February 2003): 5–17, https://pubmed.ncbi.nlm.nih.gov/12518967/.

Women rate their past performance less highly than men.

- Ernesto Reuben, "Confidence Game," Research Feature, *Ideas at Work*, November 22, 2011, https://www.ereuben.net/research/GenderLeaderOverconfidence_Ideas.pdf.

50 percent of confidence is in our control.

- Kay and Shipman, *The Confidence Code.*

Arthur Ashe quote: "Key to self-confidence is preparation"

- "Arthur Ashe: 'One Important Key to Success Is Self-confidence. An Important Key to Self-confidence Is Preparation,'" *The Socratic Method*, October 19, 2023, https://www.socratic-method.com/quote-meanings/arthur-ashe-one-important-key-to-success-is-self-confidence-an-important-key-to-self-confidence-is-preparation.

Confidence is belief in yourself . . .

- Kay and Shipman, *The Confidence Code.*

Chapter 5: Finding Confidence Through Your Inner Compass

Benefits of mindfulness

- Daniel Goleman and Richard J. Davidson, *Altered Traits: Science Reveals How Meditation Changes Your Mind, Brain, and Body* (Avery, 2017).

Mindfulness program

- Mark Williams and Danny Penman, *Mindfulness: An Eight-Week Plan for Finding Peace in a Frantic World* (Rodale, 2011).

How long does it take to see benefits of mindfulness?

- American Psychological Association, *Speaking of Psychology*, podcast, episode 131, "How Meditation Can Help You Live a Flourishing Life, with Richard Davidson, PhD," March 3, 2021, https://www.apa.org/news/podcasts/speaking-of-psychology/meditation.

Benefits of mindfulness for introverts

- Arnie Kozak, *The Awakened Introvert: Practical Mindfulness Skills to Help You Maximize Your Strengths and Thrive in a Loud and Crazy World* (New Harbinger Publications, 2015).

Four characters of the brain and intuition

- Bolte Taylor, *Whole Brain Living*.

Ted talk with Jill Bolte Taylor explaining her experience in her brain when she had a stroke

- Jill Bolte Taylor, "My Stroke of Insight," *TED Talk*, February 2008, 18 min., 21 sec., https://www.bing.com/videos/riverview/relatedvideo?q=hJill+Bolte+Taylor% 3a+My+stroke+of+insight&mid=065CD8BE314A74629167065CD8BE314A74629167&FORM=VIRE.

Purpose

- Kaufman, *Transcend.*
- Jim Loehr, *The Power of Story: Change Your Story, Change Your Destiny in Business and in Life* (Simon and Schuster, 2008).
- Mohr, *Playing Big*.

Other resources on purpose

- Tracy Brower, "Purpose May Be the Key to Happiness: 3 Reasons Why," *Forbes Magazine*, March 19, 2023, https://www.forbes.com/sites/tracybrower/2023/03/19/purpose-may-be-the-key-to-happiness-3-reasons-why/.
- Kennon M. Sheldon, "Becoming Oneself: The Central Role of Self-Concordant Goal Selection," *Personality and Social Psychology Review* 18, no. 4 (June 30, 2014): 349–65, https://doi.org/10.1177/1088868314538549.

Empathy and self-compassion

- Michael Miller and Alexandra Tanon Olsson, "Name It to Tame It: How Naming Your Emotions ("Affect Labeling") Lowers Stress and Builds Emotional Intelligence," Six Seconds, October 22, 2025, https://www.6seconds.org/2021/01/08/getting-unstuck-power-naming-emotions/.

Chapter 6: Connecting to the Wisdom Within

Inner Mentor

- Mohr, *Playing Big.*

Elder Wiser Self or Sage

- Chamine, *Positive Intelligence.*

Power of imagining yourself leads to self-improvement.

- Restak, *The Naked Brain.*

Visualizing future self leads to improved well-being and savings.

- Abraham Rutchick, Michael Slepian, Monica Reyes, Lindsay Pleskus, and Hal Hershfield, "Future Self-Continuity Is Associated with Improved Health and Increases Exercise Behavior," *Journal of Experimental Psychology Applied* 24, no. 1 (March 1, 2018): 72–80, https://doi.org/10.1037/xap0000153.
- Hal E. Hershfield, Daniel G. Goldstein, William F. Sharpe, Jesse Fox, Leo Yeykelis, Laura L. Cartstensen et al., "Increasing Saving Behavior Through Age-Progressed Renderings of the Future Self," *Journal of Marketing Research* 48, no. SPL (February 1, 2011): S23–37, https://doi.org/10.1509/jmkr.48.spl.s23.

If you speak to yourself in the third person, not first person, you will use more positive language.

- Ethan Kross, Emma Bruehlman-Senecal, Jiyoung Park, Aleah Burson, Adrienne Dougherty, Holly Shablack et al., "Self-Talk as a Regulatory Mechanism: How You Do It Matters," *Journal of Personality and Social Psychology* 106, no. 2 (January 1, 2014): 304–24, https://doi.org/10.1037/a0035173.

Connecting to the Wisdom Within visualization exercise

- Mohr, *Playing Big.*
- Chamine, *Positive Intelligence.*

Chapter 7: Tuning Out Your Critical Voice

Inner Critic

- Mohr, *Playing Big.*

Saboteurs

- Chamine, *Positive Intelligence.*

Four characters

- Bolte Taylor, *Whole Brain Living.*

Flow State

- Mihaly Csikszentmihalyi, *Flow: The Psychology of Optimal Experience* (HarperCollins, 2018).

Accept or convert it to a gift.

- Chamine, *Positive Intelligence.*

Show gratitude.

- Melissa Madeson, "The Neuroscience of Gratitude & Its Effects on the Brain," *PositivePsychology.com*, September 29, 2025, https://positivepsychology.com/neuroscience-of-gratitude/.

Chapter 8: Speaking Up

Women wanting to be liked

- Mohr, *Playing Big.*

Women speak up less often than men.

- Christopher Karpowitz, Tali Mendelberg, and Lee Shaker, "Gender Inequality in Deliberative Participation," *The American Political Science Review* 106, no. 3 (2012): 533–47, http://www.jstor.org/stable/23275432.

OARS Model

- "The OARS Model: Essential Communication Skills," Center for Health Training, National Institutes of Health (NIH), 2010, https://nida.nih.gov/sites/default/files/oarsessentialcommunicationtechniques.pdf.
- W.R. Miller and S. Rollnick, *Motivational Interviewing: Preparing People for Change*, 2nd ed., (Guilford Press, 2002).

Madeleine Albright commentary

- Meredith the Mentor, "How to Interrupt: Madeleine Albright's Best Advice for Professional Women," *Women's Agenda*, October 2, 2012, https://womensagenda.com.au/leadership/advice/how-to-interrupt-madeleine-albright-s-best-advice-for-professional-women/.

Chapter 9: Executive Presence

Executive presence is hard to define.

- Jenna Filipkowski, *Executive Presence: Desired but Ill-Defined* (Human Capital Institute, 2020), https://tracom.com/wpcontent/uploads/2020/02/HCIReportTalentPulseTRACOM.pdf.

Definition of executive presence

- Gerry Valentine, "Executive Presence: What Is It, Why You Need It and How to Get It," *Forbes*, July 31, 2018, https://www.forbes.com/sites/forbescoachescouncil/2018/07/31/executive-presence-what-is-it-why-you-need-it-and-how-to-get-it/.

Power poses and impact on confidence

- "Breaking Down Amy Cuddy's TED Talk: The Power of Power Poses," The Speaker Lab, May 3, 2024, https://thespeakerlab.com/blog/amy-cuddy-ted-talk/.
- Denise Dudley, *Work It!: Get In, Get Noticed, Get Promoted* (SkillPath Publications, 2017).

Theory of constructed emotion

- Lisa Feldman Barrett, *7 1/2 Lessons about the Brain* (HarperCollins, 2021).

Enclothed cognition—how what we wear impacts our cognition

- Hajo Adam and Adam D. Galinsky, "Enclothed Cognition," *Journal of Experimental Social Psychology* 48, no. 4 (February 21, 2012): 918–25, https://doi.org/10.1016/j.jesp.2012.02.008.

Impact of dress on behavior and hormones

- Matthew Hutson and Tori Rodriguez, "Dress for Success: How Clothes Influence Our Performance," *Scientific American*, January 1, 2016, https://www.scientificamerican.com/article/dress-for-success-how-clothes-influence-our-performance/.

Chapter 10: Visibility and Influence

"No more than my space, no less than my place"

- Alan Morinis, *Everyday Holiness: The Jewish Spiritual Path of Mussar* (Shambhala Publications, 2008).

Women's greatest impact on success is sharing achievements.

- Bonnie Marcus, "What Does It Take to Get Ahead? A Lesson from Sharon Allen," *Forbes*, October 24, 2011, https://www.forbes.com/sites/bonniemarcus/2011/10/24/what-does-it-take-to-get-ahead-a-lesson-from-sharon-allen/.

Speaking is correlated with perceived influence.

- Karpowitz, Mendelberg, and Shaker, "Gender Inequality in Deliberative Participation."

Introverts should "make the most of their own natural strengths instead of trying to act like extroverts."

- Kahnweiler, *The Introverted Leader.*

Extrovert fascination

- Kozak, *The Awakened Introvert.*

"Charisma is more about revealing what is already there . . ."

- Chung, *The Irresistible Introvert.*

Chapter 11: Networking: One Conversation at a Time

"Unwritten rule of success"

- "Sally Krawcheck Quotes," A-Z Quotes, https://www.azquotes.com/author/33621-Sallie_Krawcheck.

"Networking that matters is helping people . . ."

- "Seth Godin Quotes," A-Z Quotes, https://www.azquotes.com/quote/912827

85 percent of jobs are filled through networking.

- Steven Austin, "18 Quotes About Networking That'll Help You Connect with People," Marketing Scoop, May 13, 2024, https://www.marketingscoop.com/marketing/18-quotes-about-networking-thatll-help-you-connect-with-people/.

What is networking?

- Arnaud Belinga, "What Is Networking? (Explained with Examples)," Breakcold, October 11, 2023, https://www.breakcold.com/explain/networking.

"Sets up win-win situations"

- "Earl G. Graves, Sr. Quotes," A-Z Quotes, https://www.azquotes.com/quote/786689.

Why reciprocity feels good

- Sneha Mathur, "Why Helping Feels Good: The Neuroscience of Reciprocity," *Knowing Neurons* (blog), April 29, 2025, https://knowingneurons.com/why-helping-feels-good-the-neuroscience-of-reciprocity/.

"Everybody thinks it's making cold calls . . ."

- "Reid Hoffman Quotes," Brainy Quote, https://www.brainyquote.com/quotes/reid_hoffman_488532.

"Curiosity can spark positive feelings in the brain . . ."

- Lisa Cron, *Wired for Stories: The Writer's Guide to Using Brain Science to Hook Readers from the Very First Sentence* (Ten Speed Publishing, 2012).

"Small talk connects us and greases the gears of society."

- Sophia Dembling, *The Introvert's Way: Living a Quiet Life in a Noisy World* (Tarcher, 2012).

Chapter 12: Managing Your Energy

"Introverts need more quiet, alone time . . ."

- Stacey L. Nash, "Stress Management for Introverts: 6 Tips," Psych Central, February 24, 2022, https://psychcentral.com/stress/how-introverts-deal-with-stressful-situations#causes-of-stress.

Solitude helps you "reconnect with your sense of quiet, values, and intentions." Quiet plan, social calculator

- Kozak, *The Awakened Introvert.*

Quality friendship is just as important to health as exercise and stopping smoking.

- Julianne Holt-Lunstad, Timothy B. Smith, and J. Bradley Layton, "Social Relationships and Mortality Risk: A Meta-analytic Review," *PLOS Medicine* 7, no. 7 (July 27, 2010): e1000316, https://doi.org/10.1371/journal.pmed.1000316.

Thoreau's broad margin in life

- "Henry David Thoreau Quotations Search," The Walden Woods Project, https://www.walden.org/what-we-do/library/thoreau/quotations-search/.

Impact of lack of sleep similar to alcohol on cognition

- The National Institute for Occupational Safety and Health, "NIOSH Training for Nurses on Shift Work and Long Work Hours," CDC, March 31, 2020, https://www.cdc.gov/niosh/work-hour-training-for-nurses/longhours/mod3/08.html.

Graceful ways to say no

- Granneman, *The Secret Lives of Introverts.*

Chapter 14: Setting Your Own Direction

"I would have said no . . ."

- Shonda Rhimes, *Year of Yes: How to Dance It Out, Stand in the Sun and Be Your Own Person* (Simon & Schuster, 2015).

Definition of core values

- Jessica Koehler, "10 Core Values to Guide Behavior," *Psychology Today*, May 16, 2023, https://www.psychologytoday.com/us/blog/beyond-school-walls/202305/10-core-values-to-guide-behavior.

Values website and identify your values in a five-minute exercise

- "Personal Values: Free Online Test," https://personalvalu.es/personal-values-test.

Signature strengths and goals

- Kaufman, *Transcend.*

About the Author

JENNIFER MARCOU is a highly sought-after international coach and speaker specializing in introverted leadership. With thirty years of leadership experience at Microsoft and American Express, including roles as general manager and vice president, she has empowered hundreds of introverted professionals to elevate their confidence and impact at top global firms including Microsoft, Amazon, Google, Meta, Oracle, Qualtrics, UiPath, Zelle, American Express, Expedia, Danaher, Cepheid, Beckman Coulter, Hach, and others. Jennifer holds an MBA from NYU Stern School of Business, a bachelor of science in biology from Georgetown University, and a Professional Coach Certification from the International Coach Federation. She is the founder of Marcou Coaching and creator of the Lead with Quiet Confidence programs, which help introverts increase their success by leading authentically rather than changing who they are. Jennifer has spoken at prestigious global events such as Forbes Under 30 and Create & Cultivate and at New York University. Jennifer combines deep expertise and empathy to transform how introverts lead. To learn more, visit JenniferMarcou.com.